Success Guide to
Managerial Achievement

Success Guide to Managerial Achievement

Robin Stuart-Kotze
Rick Roskin

Reston Publishing Company, Inc.
A Prentice-Hall Company
Reston, Virginia

Library of Congress Cataloging in Publication Data

Stuart-Kotze, Robin.
   Success guide to managerial achievement.

   Bibliography: p.
   Includes index.
   1. Management.   2. Executive ability.   I. Roskin,
Rick.   II. Title.
HD31.S72   1983   658.4'09   82-23054
ISBN 0-8359-7141-4
ISBN 0-8359-7142-2 (pbk.)

©1983 by Reston Publishing Company, Inc.
A Prentice-Hall Company
Reston, Virginia 22090

10   9   8   7   6   5   4   3   2   1

Printed in the United States of America

*To two men who have been our teachers and mentors,
and who are our friends,*

Charles Margerison and Tom Watson

*and to all the managers who have participated
in the M.ach One Experience*

Contents

Preface

This isn't just another "how to improve yourself" book. It isn't a collection of shop-worn cliches which purport to be the great secrets of managerial success, such as, "Only read things once," or "Never open your mail first thing in the morning." It's a carefully thought out, well tested, and well researched approach to determining how best to manage your job, how to get the most out of the people who work for you, and how to get the best out of yourself. It forces you to look at your own strengths and weaknesses, your skills and your inabilities, your job and the people and technologies with which you have to deal. It gives you an effective method of deciding what to do, and how and when to do it. It is an eminently practical book. While it is centered on its own, unique theory, it focuses on practical skills of managing people for results. The M.ach One system presented here was developed with the help of, and is used by, a large number of managers on both sides of the Atlantic.

The book also contains a number of self-diagnostic instruments which allow the reader to examine how he or she leads others, is motivated, and makes decisions. These instruments are not intended to be detailed and definitive in the results they produce. Rather, they're intended to stimulate the reader to think more about himself or herself and how he or she thinks and manages. Because many individuals reading this book and implementing the M.ach One system in their jobs may want more detailed feedback on their managerial styles, we have included a full-length version of the Managing Style Location Test at the end of the book. This test is scored by computer and generates an extensive printout of information related to your management style. Details of how to receive this printout are included at the back of the book.

The approaches and techniques we have outlined in *Managerial Achievement* represent a positive and practical Western alternative to Japanese management style. As the final chapter points out, Japanese management methods are not particularly suited to our culture and our organizations. It's futile to try to copy what someone else does and to think that it will be equally successful. The Japanese system is not a copy of ours, although there has been some borrowing and some adaptation, and there are definite similarities in many areas. But don't be deceived—we are different, our society is different, our values are different, and our institutions and organizations are different. We can still play the game and win at it, but to do so, we need to concentrate on what *we're* good at, not what *they're* good at.

It's not easy to be an effective manager. There is probably no more varied and complex job in the world. But if you want to work at it, you *can* become a high achiever, and, if you think about it at all, you know you *should*. This book will show you how. It will require real effort on your part, but we know from experience with hundreds of managers who have worked with M.ach One that it can be done. We wish you the best of luck and success, and welcome any correspondence if you would like to tell us of your experiences with the M.ach One system.

As is the case with any book, there are a number of people whose help and contributions made everything possible. We have dedicated this book to Charles Margerison and Tom Watson, but we also want to thank the management and staff at the University of Bradford Management Centre in England, and in particular Michael Fordham and Judith Jaques. They believed in M.ach One in the early days and gave us support when we needed it. Thanks are also due Victor Johnston of the Atlantic Regional Management Training Centre, and David West of Rank Xerox. And of course, thanks to Ben Wentzell of Reston who encouraged us in the writing of the book, and Evalyn Schoppet who, in the difficult role of production editor, shepherded the book from its original state to a finished product.

And finally, thanks to all the managers who have participated in the M.ach One seminar. Your comments and suggestions have proved invaluable.

Robin Stuart-Kotze
Rick Roskin

1

The Business of Achievement

The modern history of management is a chronicle of striving to run organizations more effectively, of trying to achieve more with less, and of attempting to increase output and returns continually. But if management has one underlying goal, it is to *achieve*! That's the name of the game, no matter how it's played. No results mean no job in any position of significance. Politics, power, wheeling and dealing, all eventually have to show some positive results for the organization if a manager wants to keep his or her job. It's achievement that gives power, and it's the lack of it that saps power. When things turn bad, staff and shareholders lose their loyalty to the management they once heaped with praise.

Many factors lead to achievement. One is the *desire* to achieve. There's no substitute for a burning desire to do a great job. But there's more to achievement than that. Skill counts for more than desire or luck in the management game. If you know what to do and how to do it, and you're able to focus all your energy and attention in the right direction, your chances of success will be greatly increased. There are definitely some ways of managing that are more successful than others, and this book will show you how to find them. *YOU CAN LEARN TO BE A HIGH ACHIEVER!*

Managers who have achieved outstanding results attribute their success to certain basic factors. First, they have put a great deal of energy and effort into their jobs. Most of them believe that you can't achieve much unless you concentrate on what you're doing and work hard at it. Drive, energy, and the desire to do an outstanding job rather than a passable one are the commonly cited prerequisites for success. But, they point out, you don't have to run yourself into the ground—high achievers are also "smart" workers who plan their tasks so they won't waste valuable time and energy. Secondly, successful managers agree on the importance of setting priorities; managers have to decide what is important and what is not, and then devote their efforts to the former. They are not afraid to eliminate activities that they consider to be time wasters. Finally, all successful managers agree that the way they handle their colleagues and staff is critical to success. They all acknowledge that getting the most out of the people who work with and for them is a key factor in achieving what they want. In all but a few specialized areas, managers simply cannot go it alone.

The M.ach One system discussed in this book is based on the experience of managers, and their thinking on the critical dimensions of high achievement. It was developed through rigorous research, analysis, and testing of what managers said was reality. This process led to an integrated approach to management that takes into account *both* the knowledge managers have gained from experience *and* the information available from studies on the behavior of people at work. We've called it the M.ach One system of management. It's practical and easy to follow, *and it works*. Hundreds of managers in organizations in both North America and Europe have used it with success. The only equipment it requires is the desire to achieve more in your job and a willingness to work at it. M.ach One is designed for high achievers.

A manager's task is to get things done—to achieve a set of results. If the level of achievement is high and the results achieved are important ones, a manager has done a good job. If achievement is low or the results insignificant, the picture is very different. The challenge facing all managers, then, is to attain a high level of results in the critical areas of their jobs by utilizing the limited resources available to them at the time. We know that the ability to do this is an acquired skill and that the idea that managers are *born* effective is nonsense. The focus of this book is on the techniques, approaches, and methods of improving managerial achievement in virtually any job.

MANAGERIAL ACHIEVEMENT

Achieving results is a question of *how* you manage, not *what* you manage. Achievement is directly related to the specific behavior of the manager. Two individuals may have identical jobs, the same budgets, the same number of subordinates, and the same responsibilities, and yet end up with widely different results. Such differences in achievement are commonly attributed to luck on one side and hard work on the other, but the highly productive unit may not necessarily work any harder than the less productive unit, and while luck may be a factor, good managers don't rely on it.

What causes these differences in achievement? Trite as it sounds, the answer is working "smart," not just working hard. Achievement is the result of doing the right thing at the right time in the right circumstances. It is a matter of determining which areas of your job are the most important—that is, knowing what results are critical and where effort is most likely to produce high payoffs—and then deciding *how* to manage these areas most appropriately.

Managerial achievement can be defined as *the degree to which a manager produces a high level of results in the critical areas of his or her job*. Managerial achievement doesn't mean producing just any results; it means producing results that are important, significant, and that make a real contribution to the success of the enterprise. There is an old axiom in management that 20 percent of the energy, activity, and resources applied in a job or organization produce 80 percent of the results, while 80 percent of the energy, activity, and resources only manage to produce 20 percent of the outputs. The "20/80 rule," as it's called, can be seen operating in almost every job and organization. That's why the focus of M.ach One is on the *critical areas* of the job—the high payoff areas where results are of real significance.

But managerial achievement requires more than simply setting priorities and determining what results are important. And it requires more than technical skill and competence. It's *motivation* that infuses people with a desire to excel, *communication* that puts everyone on the right track, *decision-making* that takes more than immediate effects into account, and *leadership* that fits the needs and objectives of individuals, the organization, and the work itself. These are the key determinants of achievement in any organization.

Most of us have learned painfully that productivity still largely depends on people. Automation and computerization help to increase output, but without willing, committed employees no organization can survive the pressure of competition for long. Consider the example of Japanese management. Many in the United States are voicing admiration for Japan's high productivity, which is beating our own production levels in a variety of industries. The lesson to be learned from Japan is not a technological one, however. What Japanese managers understand, and what we seem to have forgotten, is that people make a difference. The way a manager handles people and situations is as important as the manager's knowledge or technical skill. His behavior—what he does, how he does it, how much of it he does, and when he does it—has a tremendous effect on how others act and react. It is this dimension of management that determines achievement.

The following incident illustrates how a manager can raise his or her level of achievement significantly by focusing on the basic elements that underlie the M.ach One system. The incident is based on actual experience, but the manager's name has been changed.

A CASE OF MANAGERIAL ACHIEVEMENT

John Jenkins was an area manager for a large life insurance company. As a salesman he had been a member of the million dollar club (selling in excess of a million dollars worth of premiums a year) for seven straight years, and the recruits who had trained under him were all top performers in the company. On the basis of his performance, he was promoted to area manager and made responsible for the sales and profits of a specific geographical area of the country. By special agreement, Jenkins was allowed to continue selling insurance himself, and his compensation package was made up of a combination of his salary as an area manager, commission on his own sales, and a percentage of the commissions of all sales made by his staff in the area.

He had been the top salesman in the area prior to his promotion, and he maintained that position in the first two years he held his new job. Although his own sales increased sharply each year, the overall sales of the unit actually decreased by 12 percent. However, Jenkins continued to be a highly effective trainer of new salespeople. He enjoyed working with new recruits and passing on much of his experience and knowledge to them, and there was a core of people in the company who were devoted to him. They were referred to as "John's Mafia."

Jenkins was worried, however, about his performance as a manager. He was proud of his achievements as a salesman, and boasted that he still had what it took to sell over a million dollars worth of premiums a year, but he realized that his job as area manager entailed more than simply setting a good example as a salesman. In fact, he began to question whether he should be selling as much as he was, and whether he should be devoting more time to other areas of the job. On the advice of a friend, he took two weeks off from the job, enrolled in a one-week managerial achievement course (M.ach One), and took the second week to completely rework his priorities, realign his concept of his job, and work out a plan of action for improving the performance of his unit.

Seven months later, Jenkins proudly remarked that he now spent a third less time working than he had before, that his personal sales—although much lower than they had been—were still moving at a rate that would allow him to sell a million dollars worth of premiums for the year, and that the sales of the people in his area had jumped 27 percent and looked as though they would end up 35 percent higher than the year before.

What he had done, first of all, was focus on the critical areas of his job and decide just what had to be done in those areas to achieve maximum results. In the process of doing this, he had been forced to recognize that much of his energy had been devoted to areas of relatively low payoff to the company, and that he had to cut them back, even though they were things he enjoyed doing.

Secondly, he had recognized that his own success was inextricably linked with the performance of his subordinates. He carefully examined each of his subordinate's jobs and assessed the strengths and weaknesses of the people in these jobs. He decided how to manage and motivate each of them, who to watch and control more closely, and who to give a freer rein to. And he also examined the types of decisions commonly made within his unit and decided how such decisions *should* be made and who should be involved in making them. As he describes it, he returned to work "completely physically exhausted" from the effort of rethinking his job, but "so charged up with excitement that I couldn't sleep. I just couldn't wait to get back and get things really moving."

Jenkins's efforts paid off handsomely. His relationships with all his employees, not just "John's Mafia," improved, and productivity in the unit as a whole increased sharply. Some jobs were changed significantly; some activities were simply ended, and attention was focused on doing things that would contribute most to the results of the unit. John Jenkins, a high achiever as an individual, had become a high achiever as a manager. His staff was pleased, and his superiors were delighted. Today he is a senior manager in the company and runs a high-profit, high-growth division of the business.

ARE YOU A HIGH MANAGERIAL ACHIEVER?

This book describes how you, as a manager, can achieve higher levels of results in your job. But you should be warned immediately that it will take more effort on your part than simply reading the material presented here. Like everything worthwhile in life, it requires work to become a high achiever. Before going any further, therefore, you should complete Exercise 1-1, the Managing Style Location Test (short form). It will provide you with some data that will be both interesting and helpful later on in the book. The test will not be explained at this juncture, but you will be shown how to score yourself and how to interpret your results following the discussion of leadership style in Chapter 3.

Exercise 1-1. Complete the Managing Style Location Test

The following two pages each contain a set of nine statements. Please read these statements and then, as instructed, decide which ones describe how you manage in the job you now hold.

This test is designed as a self-perception instrument and provides a measure of how you see your own behavior in your job. As it is for your own information only, please try to respond as honestly and accurately as possible.

The statements on the following two pages are arranged in the format shown below. You are asked to read statement 1, and then compare it to each of the other statements in turn (i.e. with statement 2, then 3, then 4, etc.), deciding in each instance, which of the pair of statements BEST DESCRIBES HOW YOU BEHAVE IN YOUR JOB. Circle the number of the appropriate statement as shown in the example below.

		A	B	C	D	E	F	G	H	No. of circled numbers	
1.	I enjoy work	①2	1③	①4	15	16	17	18	19	9	
2.	I help subordinates	23	24	25	26	27	28	29		8	
3.	I follow rules carefully	34	35	36	37	38	39			7	

For instance, if you look at the first line containing statement 1 "I enjoy work", you will notice that the respondent compared that statement with each of the following statements on the page and felt that statement 1 described him or her better than 2, that 3 described him or her better than 1, that 1 described him or her better than 4, etc. In other words, the respondent circled the statement in every pair that he or she felt best described his or her behavior on the job.

Please make sure you make a choice in each instance. In other words, make sure you have circled one of the pair of numbers in each box, even if it seems that neither applies to you, or that both apply to you equally. You must make a choice in every instance.

Disregard the column at the right of the page headed "No. of circled numbers". You will be given instructions concerning how to use it when you have completed all your choices.

Managing Style Location Test

		A	B	C	D	E	F	G	H
1.	I don't hesitate to criticize poor performance.	1 2	1 3	1 4	1 5	1 6	1 7	1 8	1 9
2.	I make sure the organization doesn't get the better of me.	2 3	2 4	2 5	2 6	2 7	2 8	2 9	
3.	I try to avoid arguments as much as possible.	3 4	3 5	3 6	3 7	3 8	3 9		
4.	I stay abreast of the latest developments in my field.	4 5	4 6	4 7	4 8	4 9			
5.	I like to make sure all the details in a job are tidied up properly.	5 6	5 7	5 8	5 9				
6.	I try to keep contact with the important groups in the organization.	6 7	6 8	6 9					
7.	Once I get going on something, I see it through to the bitter end.	7 8	7 9						
8.	I make sure the goals and activities of the people I work with are well coordinated.	8 9							
9.	My subordinates often come and discuss problems with me.								

No. of circled numbers (Page 1)

9	
8	
7	
6	
5	
4	
3	
2	
1	
Total: 36	

NOTE: There should only be one circled number per box.

Managing Style Location Test

		A	B	C	D	E	F	G	H		No. of circled numbers (Page 2)
1.	When I want performance I tighten the pressure on my people.	1 2	1 3	1 4	1 5	1 6	1 7	1 8	1 9	9	
2.	I sometimes "lose" memos and files just for the hell of it.	2 3	2 4	2 5	2 6	2 7	2 8	2 9		8	
3.	I try to be friends with everyone at work.	3 4	3 5	3 6	3 7	3 8	3 9			7	
4.	I find that logic can solve most problems.	4 5	4 6	4 7	4 8	4 9				6	
5.	I stick to the rules and apply them evenly to everyone.	5 6	5 7	5 8	5 9					5	
6.	I try to keep in tune with the politics of the organization.	6 7	6 8	6 9						4	
7.	I emphasize results above all.	7 8	7 9							3	
8.	I work best with a highly productive group around me.	8 9								2	
9.	I try to help my subordinates whenever necessary.									1	
										Total: 36	

NOTE: There should only be one circled number per box.

WHAT IS M.ACH ONE?

M.ach One is a system for increasing managerial achievement. It has two main dimensions: (1) it focuses on the manager's *job* and the important results that must be achieved within it, and (2) it focuses on the *behavior* the manager exhibits in getting the job done. Without a clear concept of the job and the knowledge of where effort needs to be applied to obtain high payoffs (that is, a perception of the "right" things to do in the job), and without a knowledge of how to behave in order to reach these goals, high achievement can never occur. Within these two dimensions, M.ach One focuses on how managers make decisions, communicate with employees, motivate them and lead them. Job understanding, leadership style, motivation, communication, and decision-making are interrelated components that lead to achievement.

Successful management is largely based on common sense. No books describe how to handle all the various situations that a manager faces each day of his or her working life, and no individual knows precisely how to act in every situation that arises. We all learn from experience, that is, by doing. Therefore M.ach One will not tell you how to manage, what you should do, or what the magic answer is to every problem or situation you encounter as a manager. What it will do, though, is provide you with a framework with which you can analyze jobs, identify the types of behavior that seem likely to cause the best results, clarify your approach to motivation, determine what you do well and what you do poorly, examine how you do and should make decisions, and allow you to tailor your actions and your job so as to make the most of things. It will, in short, show you how you can achieve more in your job. But always remember that *you* are the one who has to apply the approaches and techniques of M.ach One—it still takes work!

THE BASIS OF M.ACH ONE

The M.ach One system is based on the finding that there are three primary factors that underlie all managerial behavior and all managerial jobs. All managerial behavior, communication, motivation, jobs, and approaches to decision-making are concerned, to some degree, with:

- **Task-Centeredness (TC).** Emphasis on directing, initiating, controlling, and structuring of the *task* to be done.
- **Relationship-Centeredness (RC).** Emphasis on trust, listening, cooperation, encouragement, and *relationships* with others.
- **Situation-Centeredness (SC).** Emphasis on integration, organization, synthesis, and coordination of the various elements in a work *situation*.

If you think of how you behave as a manager and of how others above, beside, and below you in your organization behave, you will recognize instances of task-centeredness (giving orders, telling people what to do and when to do it, setting up organization and structure, checking on the activities of others, making unilateral decisions without consultation of any kind), of relationship-centeredness (listening to subordinates' problems, giving advice, operating an "open door" style of management, getting employee input on important decisions, encouraging, coaching, and assisting), and of situation-centeredness (coordinating, integrating, bringing conflicting parties and views together, using a consensus form of decision-making, negotiating, and planning). All managers exhibit these types of behaviors to some degree. Some managers are highly task-centered, and show little relationship-centered or situation-centered behavior. Others are highly relationship-centered and are reluctant to give direct orders or to initiate actions, while still others spend almost all of their time planning and coordinating the activities of those around them.

In talking about how managers motivate employees, communicate with them, make decisions, and generally behave toward both the people around them and their own jobs, we are essentially talking about the degree of task-, situation-, and relationship-centeredness they display in the work setting. These are the underlying bases of all management action, the common denominators to which we can reduce the vast complexity of managerial operations. Because management is such an intricate business, and because it is so difficult to master in view of the many variables present in each management situation, being able to reduce this complexity to the key underlying factors is immensely helpful.

The M.ach One system is much like the glasses used for watching 3-D movies: it transforms a blurry image that is difficult to comprehend into a picture that makes sense. M.ach One enables us to perceive what is going on and to react in an immediate and natural fashion. Like any good system or theory, M.ach One clarifies the confusing picture of managerial life and work by reducing it to its basic, understandable components.

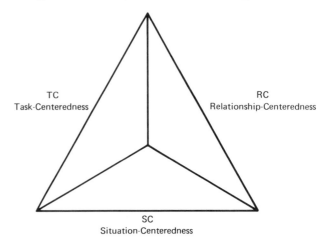

Figure 1-1. The Three Basic Dimensions of Managerial Behavior

Research shows that the dimensions of task-, situation-, and relationship-centeredness are relatively independent of one another (Figure 1-1). In other words, a manager can exhibit a high degree of, say, task-centered behavior without necessarily having to forego situation- or relationship-centered behavior. The degree to which a person uses one, or a combination, of the basic approaches to managing is largely determined by a given situation and is not based on an either-or choice.

THE JOB FOCUS

Before you can decide how to handle your job, however, you have to know what it entails. As well as being able to come to grips with motivation, management style, communication, and decision-making, managers must have a clear and straightforward method of looking at jobs and determining where they should focus their energies and attention. M.ach One has developed a simple means of doing this. By employing what is known as a "critical incident method," M.ach One has been able to identify twenty-seven elements that can be used to describe any managerial job.

We should first explain what is meant by "critical incident method." This refers to a technique whereby a large number of managers are asked to describe incidents in which their behavior led to either highly positive or highly negative outcomes. By examining these incidents and analyzing them to determine the basic managerial action involved, we can identify the types of actions that lead to success in certain situations. The twenty-seven Critical Achievement Elements used in M.ach One are the result of almost ten years of research and refinement. They represent a comprehensive list of the basic processes which, when applied appropriately, lead to achievement. Each of these elements can be related to one of the underlying bases of management, so that some are task-centered (TC), some situation-centered (SC), and some relationship-centered (RC).

In essence, then, M.ach One says that (a) a job can be analyzed in terms of the critical processes required for high achievement, and (b) that each of these processes is the result of certain types of behavior. M.ach One therefore looks at achievement from two sides—the *job* and the *behavior* of the manager. These two are linked by the fact that both of them can be described in terms of their centeredness—TC, SC, and RC. In order to attain high levels of achievement, certain critical processes must occur (job), and these processes are the result of certain types of behavior (motivation, communication, leadership, and decision-making).

The twenty-seven Critical Achievement Elements used in M.ach One to analyze managerial jobs are listed in Table 1-1. They will help you answer the question "What critical management processes will lead to high achievement in this job?" In some jobs, for instance, the critical processes might be tight *control*, accurate *forecasting*, detailed *planning*, a high standard of *quality*, and consistent *evaluation* of performance. These particular processes are the result of a largely situation-centered approach, combined with some minor degree of task-centeredness.

**Table 1-1. The Twenty-Seven Critical Achievement
Elements of M.ach One**

Task-Centered	Situation-Centered	Relationship-Centered
1. Control	10. Change	19. Advice
2. Direction	11. Coordination	20. Collaboration
3. Implementation	12. Delegation	21. Discussion
4. Motivation	13. Evaluation	22. Encouragement
5. Objectives	14. Forecasting	23. Guidance
6. Performance	15. Negotiation	24. Innovation
7. Persuasion	16. Planning	25. Listening
8. Production	17. Quality	26. Morale
9. Quantity	18. Strategy	27. Coaching

HOW CAN YOU ACHIEVE MORE AS A MANAGER?

Managerial achievement *can* be learned. Every manager can increase his or her output, and not necessarily by simply working longer hours. Bearing in mind the "20/80" rule mentioned at the beginning of the chapter—that 20 percent of effort tends to lead to 80 percent of results, and 80 percent of effort leads to only 20 percent of the results in most jobs—you, as a manager, need to concentrate on working smart rather than just plain hard. And working smart means that you must (a) know what the critical processes in your job are, and (b) know what type of behavior to apply in each situation in order to get the best results.

Working smart is what M.ach One is all about. Every manager has a finite set of resources. These resources include time, finances, equipment, space, and people. In order to be a high achiever in your job, you have to make the best use of these limited resources. If energy and attention are focused on areas that produce only 20 percent rather than 80 percent of the payoffs, achievement will, by definition, be low. Because none of the basic resources a manager has to work with are of any use by themselves without "management"—time, money, equipment, and people all have to be "managed" in one way or another—the style of a manager is critically important. If you handle people the wrong way, they won't work well for you. If you don't plan the proper use of time, money, or equipment, if you don't focus on key elements in certain situations (such as a need for high levels of quality control for certain products, or for high levels of innovation in others), if you don't set clear objectives, or provide adequate guidance to employees, if you make decisions inappropriately, or if you don't delegate enough responsibility and authority to allow people to do their jobs, you are failing to use the resources at your disposal to the best of your ability. You are not achieving what you can in your job.

You must focus on the important areas of your job and ignore the unimportant ones. Is planning important, for example? Is it very important? Is it essential? What about delegating or providing guidance, coordination, or innovation? Which of these elements are absolutely essential to doing your job well, and which are less important or unnecessary? It makes no sense to spend a great deal of time and effort on planning when the job at hand is routine and does not require much planning. Neither does it make sense to spend time telling people what they have to do and keeping a close and constant watch over them when they know their jobs and simply need to be left alone to do them. There is a wide variety of managerial jobs, and all of them require a different set of priorities. As a manager, you have to be able to determine the most important elements of your job, then focus all your time and attention on them.

But you also have to know *how* to act in order to implement these critical processes. You have to know whether a task-centered approach is the best way, or whether you should act in a more relationship-centered, or situation-centered, fashion. Some jobs require a manager to be highly directive, to initiate communication and commands, to make all the decisions on his own, to spend a lot of time and effort controlling what is going on, and to concentrate on structuring and ordering the activities of subordinates. Other jobs, however, require just the opposite. In jobs where creativity and innovation are important, or where subordinates are highly skilled specialists who know more about their jobs than the manager, a strong directive approach is counterproductive, if not explosive. What may be required is more relationship-centered or situation-centered behavior. This book will help you determine when to adopt each of these approaches.

Managerial achievement is the result of matching behavior with the requirements of the job. We will make the point a number of times: there is no best way of managing; it depends on the job. Different jobs need to be managed differently, and different people need to be managed differently. This doesn't just mean concentrating on leadership style. Leadership style is only one factor affecting achievement. Successful management involves the motivation of people, communicating with them effectively, making decisions appropriately (with more than just the bare facts in mind), and providing a model of leadership that subordinates can respond to positively. M.ach One will give you a means of analyzing your job, your people, and your approach to management, and will show you where to make adjustments so that you can focus all your energy and skill in the right way, on the right things. In short, it will help you become a high achieving manager.

2

Doing the
Right Stuff

The high achieving manager spends a lot of time deciding *what* to do. Forethought and planning are important tools of success. Success means significant results, and that means focusing all one's attention and energy on those areas where high payoffs are most likely. At a lower level, every salesman worth his or her salt knows that the bottom line is sales made, not calls made. The rookie knows that for every ten calls made you get one sale, but the veteran knows that if you plan the calls carefully, for every ten calls you get *two* sales. The same is true for management. There is a definite relationship between effort and results, but it's not a one-to-one relationship. It's less a matter of *how much* you do than *what* you do that counts.

M.ach One is concerned with doing the right things, rather than doing things right. That distinction is important. If you never stand back from your job and weigh the significance of the results of your work, you may find yourself working very hard but focusing your efforts on areas that are relatively unimportant. M.ach One is concerned with the aggressive pursuit of the things that produce major results. This involves taking some risks, taking a stand, making a commitment, and giving it your best effort. But achievement is not the result of a gung ho attitude; it also requires a clear head, cool analytical thought, and a high level of managerial skill. When Tom Wolfe talked about the astronauts having "the right stuff," he meant that they remain cool and calm under the most mind-boggling conditions and are heroes cut in a classic mold. Managers can be heroes, too. Without good managers, organizations can't survive, and nations can't survive. The job has to be done, and it has to be done well if society as a whole is to benefit.

Unfortunately, society has not figured out how to publicly reward management heroes. They are given some money and a certain degree of status, and if they're very lucky their pictures appear in *Fortune, Forbes,* or the *Wall Street Journal*, but in the final analysis, they don't get the recognition that they really deserve. If anything, they become targets for anti-business groups who argue that managers are willfully polluting, stripping, and gouging their environment and their fellow citizens. Although there are no public medals for managers, there is the great personal satisfaction of knowing when a job is done well. Achievement is extremely rewarding, and it is very important, even if it is less well recognized than it should be.

How do *you* manage your job? Do you manage it, or does it manage you? Because of the constant stream of demands in most jobs, it's very easy to spend all your time keeping your head above water and attending to tasks

19

as they occur. That keeps you abreast of the game, but it doesn't put you ahead of it. And unless you're ahead of the game, you can't afford the time to sit back and analyze and plan; you can't make sure that you have identified the *critical issues* (when you deal with things as and when they occur, everything is critical), and you can't focus appropriate resources on problems. The tendency is to devote too much time and effort to some things and not enough to others. This habit is nothing to be particularly ashamed of, because almost everybody falls into the trap at some time, but it is certainly something to avoid if you can, and something to be sheepish about if you fail to take steps to overcome it.

GETTING A FIX ON YOUR JOB

In Chapter 1 we discussed in general the alternative ways of behaving as a manager and noted that the way you communicate, motivate, lead, and make decisions has a tremendous effect on the type of results you achieve in your job. But, as you know, achievement depends on more than how you behave as a manager. All jobs are different, and what works well in one may be a disaster in another. You have to understand the requirements of the situation you're facing, and you have to identify the right actions to handle that situation before you can decide how to go about it. We can conclude, then, that job analysis is concerned with *what* to do, whereas managerial behavior is concerned with *how* to do it.

What do you do in your job? What are your most critical activities? Talking with people? Attending meetings? Talking on the telephone? Planning? Giving directions? Forecasting? Evaluating performance and results? Controlling processes and activities? Coordinating people and things? What do you do most during your day? What is your most important activity or set of activities?

Before you go any further, spend a few minutes thinking about how you handle your job on a day-to-day and week-to-week basis. Exercise 2-1 provides you with some space to note how you spend most of your time. Write down, in point form, the things you do most. (We are talking here about what you *actually* do, not what you think you *should* do.) This is a rather important step in the process of improving managerial achievement, and we strongly urge you to go through it now before you proceed further in the book. Increasing achievement is a process that takes time and effort. It's rather like running a marathon; consistent and diligent training makes the achievement possible. You can't make it without preparation.

Exercise 2-1. List the major activities in your job.

List the activities you spend most of your working day engaged in. Try to be more specific than "managing" or "communicating." For instance, you might list such things as: attending meetings, having telephone conversations, planning sales/production budgets, completing routine paperwork, etc. While you don't wish to be too vague or general, try not to be overly specific either. List the things that you do that occupy major amounts of your time and energy.

1.

2.

3.

4.

5.

6.

7.

8.

9.

As you put together your list in Exercise 2-1, you no doubt recognized a number of things that you would like to do, or would like to do more often, and also some things that you should stop doing, or should do less often. That's normal. Unless we pay constant attention to what we do every day, we will lapse into doing either what we like best, what is easiest, or what is forced on us by lack of planning. However, now that you're in the mood to think about your activities at work, why not spend a few more minutes jotting down in Exercise 2-2 what you think you should really be doing in your job in order to manage it most effectively.

21

Exercise 2-2. List the major activities that *should* be part of your job.

List those activities or processes which you feel you *should* engage in if you were to do your job in the best manner possible. You may, in fact, be doing some or all of these things now. Should you do more or less of them? Are there some things you feel you should be doing, but are prevented from for various reasons? List them, and also make a brief note of why you can't, or don't, do them.

1.

2.

3.

4.

5.

6.

7.

8.

9.

Every manager has a particular set of objectives to meet. They define his or her job. If you want to know what an individual's job is, you are better off asking what it is that has to be achieved in the job rather than asking what the job title is. For instance, what do the titles "assistant administrative officer" or "account supervisor" mean? Do they describe the jobs of people who assist administrative officers, or who supervise accounts? They might, and they might not. Account supervisors can be anything from accountants to salesmen to branch managers, and administrative officers are just about as ubiquitous and varied in what they do. To define a job, one has to know what it's supposed to produce, what its hoped-for results or objectives are. When we talk about "the job" in this book, we mean *the organizational outputs over which a manager has formal authority and responsibility*. In other words, your job can best be thought of as what you are expected to achieve.

Jobs change over time. That is to say, the goals over which a manager has formal authority and responsibility change, and the corresponding outputs, processes, and activities change. For high achievement to occur, you have to have a constant fix on your job. You have to know what it requires now in terms of outputs and activities. Managers who do not have a clear picture of their jobs tend to manage them inappropriately; they may do things that are no longer necessary or may focus on unimportant aspects of the job. What is needed, therefore, is a simple, straightforward method of analyzing a job to identify its critical elements. If we can also determine what managerial behavior is appropriate in dealing with these elements, achievement should result. The M.ach One system does both of these things through the *Critical Achievement Element Pool* mentioned in Chapter 1.

ANALYZING THE JOB BASIS

Each job within an organization demands a particular type of managerial behavior. Some aspects of a job are more important than others and could be considered critical to effective performance. A job can be said to consist of three separate yet interrelated parts. The first is *outputs*, or what the job is intended to achieve. These are the results by which achievement is judged. They should be differentiated from *processes*, which are the basic types of managerial activity required to achieve outputs. Finally, a job is made of *priorities* that define *order* and *emphasis* of both output and process requirements.

Once you, as a manager, clearly understand the boundaries of your responsibilities (your required goals, or outputs), you can start acting. What is to be achieved usually requires some input from a higher level; how to achieve it is best decided by the individual in the job.

As we talk about analyzing the job, we assume that the manager knows his or her basic goals. You have to know where you're going before you set off to get there. The basic goals in a job reflect organizational policy. Are we primarily interested in quality or quantity of product? Is our goal market share, return on assets, or equity? Are we concerned with creativity and one-off inventions or developments, or are we interested in producing a standard product at the lowest possible cost? These are some of the organizational questions that must be answered before a manager can determine how to do his or her job better.

As noted in Chapter 1 (Table 1–1), M.ach One has identified twenty-seven management processes that lead to achievement. These twenty-seven Critical Achievement Elements (CAE's) represent a checklist of potential avenues to high payoffs that you, as a manager, should consider when you are assessing how to handle your job. These elements, we know from experience, lead to managerial achievement. Of course, you cannot and should not focus on all of them simultaneously. No job is that broad (at least no *manageable* job). But every job entails some of these elements, and failure to recognize which ones are relevant and which irrelevant leads to disaster.

To analyze his or her job, a manager simply has to examine this list of elements and choose those that best describe what actions will ensure the job is done effectively. Any job can be described by its Critical Achievement Elements. To test this method of job analysis, take the time right now to analyze your own job according to the instructions in Exercise 2-3.

Exercise 2-3. List the Critical Achievement Elements of your job

First, identify the job that you are going to analyze (either the job you now have, one you are going to move into in the near future, or one you have just left, depending on your circumstances). Then look at the Critical Achievement Element Pool and ask yourself "Which of the 27 elements best describe what must occur if a high level of achievement is to be obtained in this job?" List the appropriate ones in the space provided, noting whether each is task-centered, situation-centered, or relationship-centered.

Critical Achievement Elements

Task-Centered	Situation-Centered	Relationship-Centered
1. Control	10. Change	19. Advice
2. Direction	11. Coordination	20. Collaboration
3. Implementation	12. Delegation	21. Discussion
4. Motivation	13. Evaluation	22. Encouragement
5. Objectives	14. Forecasting	23. Guidance
6. Performance	15. Negotiation	24. Innovation
7. Persuasion	16. Planning	25. Listening
8. Production	17. Quality	26. Morale
9. Quantity	18. Strategy	27. Coaching

The Critical Achievement Elements of Your Job

Centeredness TC SC RC	Critical Achievement Element

SETTING PRIORITIES AND
RELATING THEM TO MANAGEMENT STYLE

Although a job may be adequately described by several process elements, seldom are all of these elements equally important for high achievement. Some will be essential, others important, and still others will merely put icing on the cake. In any job and any organization there is a finite amount of time, energy, and resources that can be allocated to a project. Since perfection is rarely attainable, you do the best you can and leave it at that. Therefore, priorities must be established and adhered to.

In every job some elements are absolutely essential to high achievement. Without them one simply cannot do a first-class job. For instance, one essential element in the space shuttle program is *quality* control, because certain malfunctions simply cannot be tolerated. To a brand manager in charge of introducing a new product in a competitive market, it is most important to have a clear *strategy*. Product managers in the drug industry or in the electronics business must focus primarily on *innovation*. Certain processes, then, are always critical to success in certain jobs. They must be made the top priority items in any analysis of these jobs.

Of course, a host of other things are important in all jobs, but are not absolutely essential to effectiveness. It's difficult to rank these elements because most people define actions as either essential or unnecessary, with no levels in between. But there certainly are top-priority elements and second-priority elements in every job. If you have chosen eight or nine achievement elements and believe they are all absolutely critical to success, you might just have explained that ulcer of yours, or your high blood pressure, or the demise of the person who held the job before you.

Finally, some aspects of many jobs are not critical at all. These may be things we like to do rather than have to do, or they may be the processes that turn a very good result into an exceptional one. They are the finishing touches of excellence. Of course, it's extremely satisfying to put these finishing touches on a job, as the expert craftsman will tell you when he finishes a delicate and flawless piece of work. The final finish he puts on a piece doesn't affect its function or design, and may not change its value greatly, but it does make it look just that much better. If you have the time and the resources to attend to these finishing touches, all the better, but take a long, hard look at them to make sure they aren't using resources that would be better applied elsewhere to solve more fundamental problems. The question we, as managers, must ask is whether the time and effort involved in putting this extra "finish" on a job leads to an appropriate payoff.

If you accept the 20/80 rule, then you will want to focus only on the *essential* elements of your job, since they produce optimum results. Follow the instructions in Exercise 2-4 to determine those elements which are critical to the performance of your job, and to see how these elements determine the management style necessary for maximum achievement. The sample job analysis shown in Figure 2-1 on page 29 is provided to assist you in completing your own job analysis.

Exercise 2-4. Analyze your job basis

STEP 1: Examine the elements you listed in Exercise 2-3 as being critical to effective performance in your job, and pare the list down to the nine most important ones. You probably listed more than nine originally—most people do. If, as is less common, you listed fewer than nine elements, you should go back over the list and bring your total to nine. The number nine is chosen for several reasons, primarily because experience shows that most managers need nine categories to describe their jobs adequately. Those who list more than nine elements tend to include items that are not critical to performing the job effectively, while those who have chosen fewer elements tend to have an oversimplified view of their jobs.

STEP 2: Study the nine elements you chose and decide which ones are absolutely essential for high achievement (top priority), which are important (medium priority), and which are desirable for one reason or another (low priority). Arrange the elements in descending order of priority on the analysis form provided on the following page.

STEP 3: Note whether each of the elements you have chosen is task-centered, situation-centered, or relationship-centered by placing a checkmark in the appropriate space in the column marked centeredness.

STEP 4: Note the double line between the boxes in the "Priority" column. To make it easier to see which process elements are top priority, which are medium priority, and which are low priority, simply shade in the area below each priority group of elements. For instance, if the first four elements you have listed are essentials (top priority), the next three are medium priority, and the last two are the lowest priority, you should shade in the double line between the fourth and fifth elements, and between the seventh and eighth, separating and highlighting each group. The example in Figure 2-1 illustrates this process.

STEP 5: Assign a numerical weight to each of the priority groupings. Top priority elements get a weight of 3, medium-priority elements get a weight of 2, and low priority elements get a weight of 1. Record the weight of each element in the column headed "Priority".

STEP 6: Add the priority weights of all the task-centered elements, situation-centered elements, and relationship-centered elements, respectively, and put these totals in the box headed "Total Priority Weights."

Centeredness			Critical Achievement Elements	Priority
TC	SC	RC		

Total	Priority	Weights
TC	SC	RC

Conversion Table				
Total Weight	0–1	2–6	7–9	10–27
Degrees	0	1	2	3

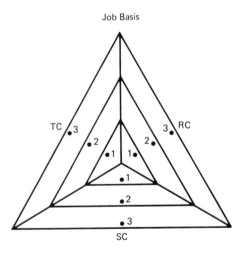

Job Basis

| Centeredness | | | Critical Achievement Elements | Priority |
TC	SC	RC		
√			Production	3
√			Quantity	3
√			Control	3
	√		Planning	3
	√		Quality	2
	√		Coordination	2
		√	Coaching	2
√			Motivation	1
		√	Discussion	1

| Total | Priority | Weights |
TC	SC	RC
10	7	3

Conversion Table				
Total Weight	0–1	2–6	7–9	10–27
Degrees	0	1	2	3

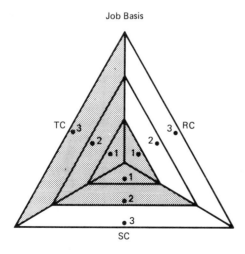

Figure 2-1. **Example of a Production Manager's Job Analysis**

STEP 7: Convert these totals, using the conversion table presented on the form, to "degrees" of TC, SC, and RC. For example, the production manager in Figure 2-1 has a total priority weighting of 10 for TC, 7 for SC, and 3 for RC. When these raw scores are applied to the conversion table, TC becomes 3 (degrees), SC becomes 2 (degrees), and RC becomes 1 (degree).

STEP 8: Each segment of the Job Basis triangle is divided into three parts, which are used to indicate the "degree" of TC, SC, or RC being represented. For instance, if we wish to show a very small amount of, say, RC (and we refer to a small amount as 1 degree of it), we would shade in the portion of the RC segment of the triangle, starting at the middle point, and ending at the line marked 1 degree, as in Figure 2-1. If we want to show a moderate amount of a basic centeredness, say SC, we would shade in 2 degrees in that segment (once again, as in Figure 2-1). And if we wish to indicate a very high level of a certain centeredness, we would shade in the entire segment (for example, the TC segment in Figure 2-1, where the manager's job requires 3 degrees of task-centeredness).

In essence, the Job Basis triangle portrays in graphic form the *underlying behavioral requirements of the job*—that is, in general, the type of behavior that is needed to do the job properly. *This is the link between management style and the job*! So now we have a means of looking at a job in terms of the types of functions or processes necessary to do it well, and these, in turn, indicate *how* to manage the job (in terms of communication, motivation, leadership and decision-making). In other words, our method of analysis tells us how to be high achievers in specific jobs.

SUMMARY

The M.ach One system is a dual approach to managerial achievement. Achievement is the result of doing the right things in the right situation; a manager must be aware of his or her type of behavior on the job and at the same time must have a clear concept of the critical processes required to complete the job satisfactorily. Jobs are made up of a number of elements, some of which are more important to achievement than others. Unless the priorities are made clear, time and energy can easily be misplaced. The result is, to quote Shakespeare, a lot of "sound and fury, signifying nothing."

A great deal of attention is paid to how managers behave in their jobs. Because behavior is a personal issue, it is of interest to everyone, and because managers interact with other people all day long, what they do is noticed. Because the job is less glamorous and less exciting, it is of less interest, or, at best, is given lip service when job descriptions are updated. As all managers know, the problem with job descriptions is that they either get filed away and forgotten, or else they become instruments for limiting what an individual does. Whenever relations between management and employees are poor, job descriptions tend to be used as a threat by the employees. "Work to rule" has nonproductive connotations.

The critical processes required to do a job well are sometimes difficult to pinpoint. They take a lot of careful thought. Discussing the issue with co-workers often helps to identify them. Time and effort spent in defining the elements that are likely to lead to high achievement in a job have big payoffs. If you zero in on the correct elements and place the right priorities on them, then success becomes largely a matter of the amount of energy you devote to the job. Once you know the right things to do, the path to managerial achievement is clear.

3

Achievement
Is in Style

If you ask any manager to name the most important aspect of his or her job—that is, the single component that makes the greatest impact on productivity, morale, cost, or innovation—the answer is almost invariably leadership. Leadership is concerned with getting people to do things. It may involve persuasion, coordination, initiation, coercion, or even setting a good example for others to follow. Whatever the method, a manager is expected to get the job done through other people.

Throughout history, great leaders have been great achievers. Alexander the Great, Julius Caesar, Charlemagne, Napoleon, Lincoln, and Churchill all achieved monumental feats, but, obviously, none of them did it alone. The gift of all these individuals was leadership. They were able to convince large numbers of people to follow them, carry out their ideas, and implement their policies and plans. No society and no organization survives without leadership. The path through life is constantly beset by the winds of change, and the leaderless very soon lose their way.

Managers have long been concerned with leadership and what makes one individual more effective than another. Early studies of leadership tried to enumerate the characteristics of the great figures in history to determine the basic ingredients of effective leadership. Unfortunately, the characteristics were so many that it would be impossible to remember them all, let alone imitate them. The problem is that different leaders exhibit different traits. Churchill was a very different man from Lincoln, and Lincoln was very different from Caesar. And certainly none of these men approached Christ, who, in terms of numbers of followers alone, must be ranked as an exceptionally successful leader.

Successful managers, too, tend to be different from one another. Consider the differences between the great Alfred Sloan, Harold Geneen, and Ray Kroc. All the research on leadership has failed to turn up any universal traits of effective managers. Although there does not seem to be an ideal method of leadership, the way a manager operates is still recognized as a critical factor in achieving success. If there is no universal method of leading, and yet leadership is the key to organizational success, where does that leave us? The answer, of course, lies in the job a manager has to do.

MANAGEMENT STYLE

Most discussions of management style have centered on whether it is better for a manager to be directive or participative in the management of people.

Various terms have been used to refer to these basic approaches: autocratic vs. democratic; boss-centered vs. employee-centered; theory X vs. theory Y; or task-centered vs. people-centered. Nonetheless, the main issue remains whether a manager should keep close control over the work of subordinates and tell them precisely what to do, or whether he should delegate authority and responsibility, inform employees of the big picture, and let them get on with their work with a minimum of direct supervision. Academics and researchers tend to favor the latter approach, claiming that, in the long run, it produces higher levels of results. Many practicing managers, on the other hand, believe that in the long run we'll all be dead, so productivity and results should be achieved right now. Therefore, they say, you must take control of the situation and make sure people do what they're supposed to do, when they're supposed to do it.

The research conducted on the relative merits of these two approaches—let's call them *task-centeredness* and *relationship-centeredness*—indicates that one approach works well in some cases, while the other works well in others. The problem is that in certain instances neither a purely task-centered approach nor a purely relationship-centered approach appears to produce optimal results. An important component is missing from this model.

The third major factor underlying managerial style is *situation-centeredness*—a significant number of managerial jobs require a bringing together of functions, technology, and people through a process of integration, organization, synthesis, and coordination. There is no doubt that task-centered and relationship-centered behavior are major bases of managerial style. Nor is there any lack of understanding among managers that in most jobs a delicate balance of these two factors leads to high achievement. But there is more to management than driving people sometimes and stroking them at other times; often you have to bring their activities and energies together. A manager's job is like the role of the conductor of a symphony orchestra; he has to coordinate and integrate the efforts and skills of a large number of people, all of whom know their own jobs and can perform them well, but need to be fitted into a grand design in order to be able to produce the final product. Style must therefore take into account what we refer to as the *situation*—the job to be done and the resources, people, technology, time, and so on a manager has at his or her disposal to do it.

SITUATION-CENTEREDNESS

The M.ach One system sprang from research into this third factor of managerial behavior. It is the first management theory to recognize situation-centeredness as a major component of managerial style. The M.ach One system associates managerial behavior with task-centeredness (TC), relationship-centeredness (RC), *and situation-centeredness* (SC). All management behavior can be described in terms of the degree to which it is concerned with these three factors. Since these approaches are largely independent of one another, being highly task-centered, for instance, does not preclude one from being highly concerned with relationships, or behaving in a situation-centered manner. You don't have to be one or the other—you can, and often will, use a combination of the three approaches simultaneously.

These three underlying components of managerial behavior can be represented diagrammatically, as shown earlier in Figure 1-1. Each of the sides of the basic triangle represents either task-centeredness (TC), situation-centeredness (SC), or relationship-centeredness (RC). The reason we use a triangle is because, although the three factors TC, SC, and RC are largely independent, research has shown that they do have *some* relationship to one another, and therefore should not be represented at right angles to one another. The triangular diagram thus expresses the *relative* independence of the three factors, but also reflects the fact that there is some interrelationship between them. The basic style model is shown in Figure 3-1.

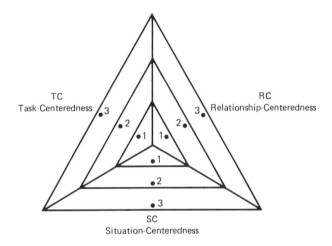

Figure 3-1.   The Basic Style Triangle

A manager's basic style—that is, the degree of TC, SC, and RC he or she manifests through behavior—can be plotted on the basic style triangle. Each third of the triangle is divided into segments that reflect the amount of the specific approach (TC, SC, RC) underlying the manager's style. The segments are labeled in "degrees"—a factor of 3 indicates a high degree of the type of behavior, 2 a moderate degree, 1 a low degree, and 0 indicates such a small amount of the type of behavior that it is difficult to measure. Examples of this diagrammatic representation of basic style are presented in Figure 3-2. Triangle (a) shows a manager who is highly task- and relationship-centered (3 of each), but whose behavior manifests only a very small degree of situation-centeredness (1). The second manager, whose style is represented by triangle (b), is moderately situation-centered, with a low degree of task- and relationship-centered behavior. The third manager, who is represented by triangle (c), is totally relationship-centered, and exhibits virtually no task- or situation-centeredness.

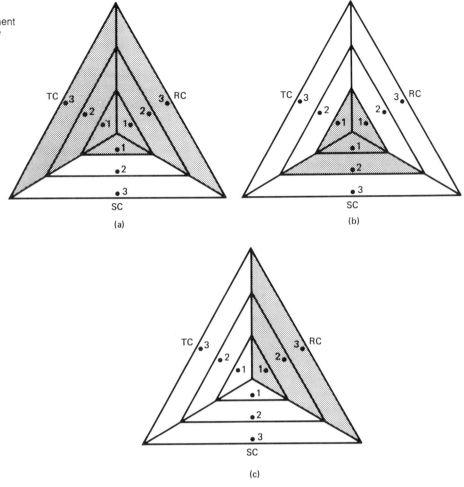

Figure 3-2. Three Examples of Style Basis Represented Visually

How we determine the degree of TC, SC, or RC a manager exhibits in his or her behavior will be explained later. At this juncture, all we need to understand is that a manager's basic behavior can be recognized and visually represented. That is, we can estimate how task-, situation-, or relationship-centered a manager is and then represent that style in diagrammatic form.

Being able to recognize a manager's underlying style, be it that of another manager or yourself, is useful because it enables you to understand what is going on around you. People react to different styles differently. We react quite differently to a highly task-centered style of behavior than we do to a highly relationship-centered one. If we can understand an individual's behavior, then we have a greater chance of being able to understand and control our reactions to it. Such an understanding will help us shift our own managerial behavior from an emotional to a more rational level.

MANAGEMENT STYLE AND ACHIEVEMENT

Although it is useful to know the basis of a manager's style, we also want to be able to determine how effective the manager is in the application of that basic style. This added dimension with which M.ach One is concerned is *managerial achievement*, defined as *the degree to which a manager produces a high level of results in the critical areas of his or her job.* We all know managers who are highly task-centered, yet some of them achieve a great deal while others arouse nothing but hostility from those who work around them. Clearly, there is a positive and negative side to any style. For instance, a manager who exhibits a high degree of relationship-centeredness (RC) in his behavior, and who uses it to achieve positive results (development of subordinates, stimulation of creativity) can be thought of as having a "positive" style, while another manager who exhibits an equally high degree of RC, but does it in a "negative" fashion (trying hard to be liked by everyone, avoiding conflict at all costs) has a style that is obstructive, if not destructive. The former manager achieves a great deal, whereas the latter achieves little or nothing.

The M.ach One system contains nine managerial styles, three of which are highly productive (positive), three of which are moderately productive and tend to maintain the status quo (neutral), and three of which are counterproductive (negative). These three achievement dimensions are illustrated in Figure 3-3.

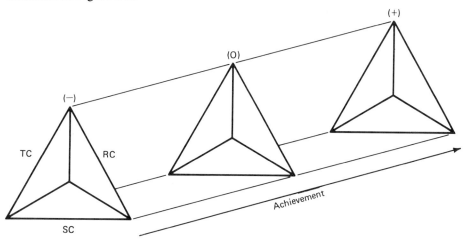

Figure 3-3. The Three Achievement Dimensions of M.ach One

To make the system easier to work with, we have labelled each of the nine managerial styles according to their style basis and achievement dimension, as shown in Table 3-1. For instance, a manager who exhibits a positive relationship-centered style is labeled an "Instructor," while relationship-centeredness that has a negative effect is given the label of "Emissary."

Table 3-1. The Nine M.ach One Management Styles

Style	Style Basis/ Achievement Dimension
Benevolent Autocrat (BA)	TC +
Technocrat (T)	TC 0
Autocrat (A)	TC −
Professional (P)	SC +
Bureaucrat (B)	SC 0
Defector (D)	SC −
Instructor (I)	RC +
Diplomat (DP)	RC 0
Emissary (E)	RC −

It must be recognized that no manager is likely to fit the stereotype of any one of the nine style types perfectly. Rather, each of the styles can be recognized to some degree in all types of managers. The usefulness of style profiles is that they provide a basis of comparison—a set of "mug shots" against which we can compare ourselves with others. An individual's style will not be perfectly reflected by one picture. Like the parts of a composite photograph, different elements from different style descriptions will be pieced together to make a picture of the manager concerned.

Figure 3-4 further illustrates the nine M.ach One management styles.

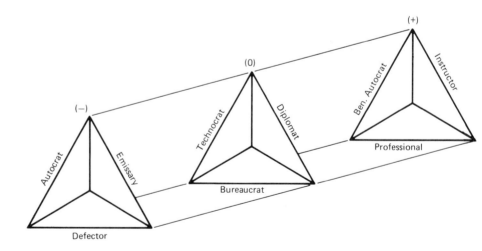

Figure 3-4. The Nine M.ach One Managerial Styles

A Reminder

Before you read further, did you complete the Management Style Location Test in Exercise 1-1? If not, please do so now, because it is concerned with your specific management style. The scoring key is given in Exercise 3-1. This exercise will provide you with a profile of the managerial styles you tend to use *in the job you now have.* The test results reflect the responses you made. If you are not sure about your responses, take the time to go over the test now and make sure you answered as intended.

Once you have scored yourself, read the capsule descriptions of each management style. You will then be able to interpret your results. You may be surprised, delighted, or even a little hurt. You may discover things about yourself that you hadn't suspected, or you may confirm things that you already knew. Whatever the results, you will have taken the first step toward becoming a high achiever. As we have said, you have to know where you are before you can decide where you want to go. Understanding how you behave as a manager is most important; it gives you the data with which to decide what you want to continue doing and what you want to change. But don't be hasty! You will need to know more about motivation, about decision-making, about communication and, of course, about your job. But that all comes later. For now, let's take a brief look at each of the management styles to get a general idea of what they are. Full descriptions are found in Appendix 1 if you want to pursue the matter of styles further at this point.

Exercise 3-1. Score and analyze your Managing Style Location Test

Before continuing with the instructions below, make sure you have circled one number in every box in Exercise 1.

INSTRUCTIONS

STEP 1: Fill in the boxes headed "No. of circled numbers" on the right-hand side of the statement page by doing the following:

- Count the number of times you have circled each number, from 1 to 9—i.e. the number of circled "1's", "2's", "3's", etc. —and mark the totals in the appropriate boxes.

  For instance, if you circled the number 1 eight times, write "8" in the box marked 1 (at the bottom of the column). If you circled the number 2 six times, write a "6" in the box marked 2; if you circled the number 3 five times, write "5" in the box marked 3; and so on.

- Fill in each of the boxes in the columns headed "No. of circled numbers."

STEP 2: Total the numbers you have written in each "No. of circled numbers" column. The total should be 36, as there are 36 possible choices to be made on each statement page. If your figures do not total 36 for each page, check your response sheet for errors.

STEP 3: Transfer the numbers in each of the "No. of circled numbers" columns to the conversion table.

STEP 4: Total the two numbers across each row of the conversion table and enter these totals in column 3.

STEP 5: The numbers in column 3 of the conversion table show the relative emphasis you place on each of nine managerial styles. The higher the number, the more you use the style. The lower the number, the less you tend to use it. Circle the two highest scores in column 3. These are your major managerial styles.

Capsule descriptions of the nine managerial styles are given after the exercise.

	Column 1		Column 2		Column 3	Managerial Style
	No. of circled numbers page 1		No. of circled numbers page 2		(Col. 1 + Col. 2)	
Row 1	9		9			Instructor (I)
Row 2	8		8			Professional (P)
Row 3	7		7			Benevolent Autocrat (BA)
Row 4	6		6			Diplomat (DP)
Row 5	5		5			Bureaucrat (B)
Row 6	4		4			Technocrat (T)
Row 7	3		3			Emissary (E)
Row 8	2		2			Defector (D)
Row 9	1		1			Autocrat (A)
	Total: 36		Total: 36		Total: 72	

THE NINE M.ACH ONE MANAGEMENT STYLES

The following capsule descriptions will give you an idea of the nine M.ach One management styles. Bear in mind that the style descriptions are like caricatures; they highlight the outstanding features of an individual rather than depicting an exact likeness. But they indicate the real flavor of each type of managerial behavior. When you are assessing your own style or someone else's, don't feel that every indicator must apply. You will be able to recognize most of the style descriptions in everyone—the question is how many of them you recognize.

We have presented the styles according to their basic centeredness. Thus we start off by looking at all the task-centered styles, describing how task-centeredness manifests itself in a positive, high-achievement fashion, a neutral fashion, and a negative, low-achievement fashion. We look at the three situation-centered styles and the three relationship-centered styles in the same way.

For grammatical ease we have used the pronoun "he" throughout the style descriptions. Should you, as a female reader, feel slighted when the positive styles are described with reference solely to males, bear in mind that the less flattering negative styles are also described that way. Fortunately (or unfortunately, depending on how your style turns out), our research shows no gender-determined management style. Managers are managers, and whether you're male or female, you still have to get the job done.

The Task-Centered Styles

BENEVOLENT AUTOCRAT (TC +). The Benevolent Autocrat is task-centered and is a high achiever. His prime concern is the completion of any job under

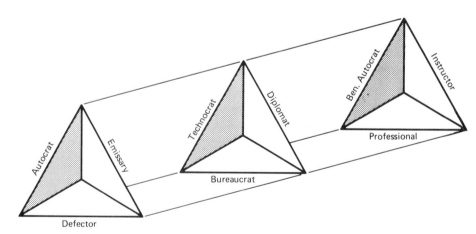

Figure 3-5. The Task-Centered Styles

his direction. Subordinates sometimes see the Benevolent Autocrat as having a concern for people, but this concern usually takes the form of paternalism, and he exhibits little real openness to the ideas of others. He is firm with people, but is able to engender loyalty and commitment. Subordinates tend to follow his lead with little question. He is completely confident in his ability to get the job done, but less confident in the people around him. As a result, he structures work and attempts to decrease interpersonal relationships. He is concerned with status symbols and other formalized procedures that determine interaction patterns. He tends to "sell" his ideas. He is motivated by the desire to complete his job successfully, no matter what, and if he has to push people out of the way to do so, he will.

Key behavioral cues for the Benevolent Autocrat are:

Dominant	Determined
Convincing	Initiator
Compelling	Results focus
Firm	Challenge-oriented
Resolute	

TECHNOCRAT (TC 0).   The Technocrat is task-centered, but is a moderate rather than a high achiever. He is, however, more effective than the Autocrat in that he is more subtle in introducing his one-sided philosophy. He often hides behind various statistical and technological data, convincing people that his arguments have merit. He is usually cool, calm, and collected. Normally ultra-prepared, he is a hard person to argue against. Subordinates or co-workers often rationalize any hostility they feel toward his actions as being a fault of the technology in general, rather than him personally. The Technocrat might be more effective if he did not make people feel so replaceable. Sometimes he creates fear in others when he pushes for new methods and ideas they don't fully understand.

The Technocrat's motivation is variable—sometimes he is motivated to help the organization, while at other times he is motivated to satisfy his own whims. He prefers to interact with technology rather than people. He is often happiest when left alone with machines and data.

The prevalence of this management style is growing, due to rapid advances in technology. The result, in many cases, is a fragile equilibrium of opposing forces between the status quo (the so-called organizational establishment) and the young, technically trained graduates who are armed with new concepts and techniques that may be threatening to those persons unfamiliar with them.

Key behavioral cues for the Technocrat are:

Logical	Knowledgeable
Rational	Technical focus
Unemotional	Single-minded
Prepared	Orderly

AUTOCRAT (TC −).   The Autocrat is task-centered, but a low achiever. He has a single purpose—to get the job done at almost any expense. It should be noted that his task-centeredness is focused on what *he* wants to have done, rather than what the organization wants to have done, and his behavior is more a manifestation of his personality than a response to the needs of the situation. People are of interest to him only insofar as they can further his goals. This single-mindedness and insensitivity to others is ineffective in the long term because people will only work for him when the pressure is great enough, and will tend to slack off when he is not pressuring them. The net result is not conducive to organizational achievement.

The Autocrat is a bully. Unlike the Benevolent Autocrat who is able to command loyalty and commitment from subordinates, the Autocrat simply engenders fear and dislike. He is highly self-oriented. His behavior focuses on achieving his own goals over those of the organization. (This statement is true of all the managers who exhibit the negative styles—Autocrat, Emissary, and Defector. These styles tend to be dominated more by personality rather than by the situation, and that, of course, is what makes them ineffective.)

In the Autocrat's view, people dislike work and must be pressured or punished to make them perform. Any decrease in expected results implies an increase in threats and demands. "Shape up or ship out" is his motto. He does not believe that a subordinate can be motivated enough to work by himself without close direction.

Key behavioral cues for the autocrat are:

Censuring	Demanding
Hard Taskmaster	Bully
Pressuring	Insensitive
Dictatorial	Uses Ultimatums

The Situation-Centered Styles

PROFESSIONAL (SC +).   The Professional is a high achiever who views his job as "getting things done through people." His situation-centeredness is manifested by a great deal of effort toward integration, coordination, and synthesis of the efforts of others. He is highly concerned about people and about getting the job done well, and he becomes deeply involved in his efforts to ensure that both these aspects of work are handled properly. He is a good delegator, listener, and team player, yet will make decisions himself when required.

The Professional is more interested in establishing strategy and achieving group results than demonstrating individual brilliance. He sets high standards and demands a great deal from himself and those who work with him. He recognizes that a manager must be sensitive to the demands of the job at all times. He sees his function, to a large degree, as the blending

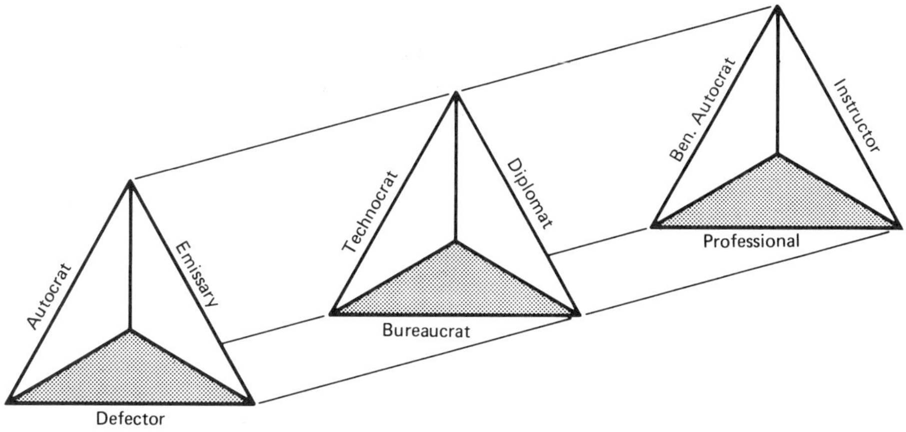

Figure 3-6. The Situation-Centered Styles

of people, skills, and technology to achieve organizational goals. He believes that people can enjoy work and that they find high levels of achievement rewarding. Although he is essentially team-oriented, the Professional is careful to treat people as individuals with unique skills and abilities. However, he attempts to structure activities so that achievement is a product of a team effort from which all members can derive satisfaction. He uses knowledge rather than tenure or rank as the criterion for determining who should do what, and has little concern for status. He is not afraid to take a firm stance and to assume a more directive leadership style when necessary.

Key behavioral cues for the Professional are:

High standards	Coordinates
Integrates	Strategy-focused
Situation-sensitive	Fair
Team player	Assured

BUREAUCRAT (SC 0). The Bureaucrat is placed at a neutral level of achievement within the M.ach One system because, although he can often get things done, he does not inject the spark of commitment, creativity, and desire that the Professional does. His situation-centeredness is focused on a clear knowledge of rules and procedures and how and when to apply them. He always plays by the rules and is highly concerned about maintaining proper procedure. In fact he is "ruled" by the rules. The Bureaucrat is intrinsically concerned neither with task achievement nor with personal relationships unless they fall within the prescribed bounds of his job. He is more concerned with doing things right than doing the right things.

Although the Bureaucrat's style does not engender high growth, innovation, and dazzling results, it is a stable, anchoring force that provides the organization with a solid foundation. The Bureaucrat does what has to be done, and does it the "proper" way. He is dogged, steadfast, and reliable (although some say he is stubborn, obstinate, and obstructive). His organizing ability often helps others to be highly effective. Without people like him to maintain systems, few organizations would be able to function.

Key behavioral cues for the Bureaucrat are:

Rational	Impersonal
Careful	Consistent
Fastidious	Conservative
Loyal	Detail emphasis
System bound	Routine focus

DEFECTOR (SC −). The Defector, although physically present, is mentally absent. He is a situation-centered nonachiever. The situation-centeredness is concerned with the defector's *own* situation, not the organization's, but his skill at sensing what is going on around him and manipulating it to his own ends should not be underestimated. This is a situation-centered style because the Defector has to be highly aware of all elements of the organization in order to continue to get away with doing nothing. The negative aspect of his style centers on his attitude of not giving a damn for the organization. He is there to remain warm in the winter, cool in the summer, and to get what he can without having to give anything in return.

Defectors are far more common in large organizations than small ones, probably because there is less available cover to hide behind in the latter. The Defector needs to be able to give the impression of being concerned and working hard when in fact he is doing just the opposite. He is least damaging when he is content to do nothing, and most damaging when he takes out his frustrations and resentment by blocking and sabotaging the plans and actions of others. The Defector is introspective, and usually sees himself as having been cheated by the organization, and even by life in general. Frequently he is correct. Most Defectors have suffered some major setback in their organizational careers that they feel unable to overcome. Although this may have soured them on life within their organizations, they are often active on the outside in clubs, charities, the church, or various hobbies. Defectors are made, not born, and sometimes they can be changed back into high achievers.

Key behavioral cues for the Defector are:

Uninterested	Disillusioned
Unmotivated	Irresponsible
Uncommitted	Bitter
Uncooperative	Devious

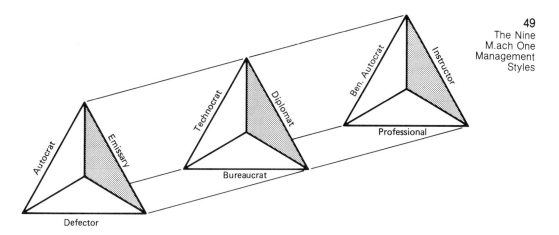

Figure 3-7. The Relationship-Centered Styles

The Relationship-Centered Styles

INSTRUCTOR (RC +).   The Instructor is a relationship-centered high achiever. His outlook is a long-term one; he trains people for future positions. He turns people with high technical skills into managers. His main interest is the development of others and, through this, the growth of the organization. His approach may be difficult to detect and so his ability sometimes goes unrewarded, but the success of his "pupils" is his recompense. Elements of this style should be found in every manager, but many fear for their own organizational lives and would prefer to be indispensable. Thus, they refuse to train people to take over their function. This is a rather frustrating circumstance for subordinates, who must jump over such a person, or move laterally, to succeed.

With the training and learning thrust of many modern organizations, the style of the Instructor will become more highly valued. Although formal training programs and "tours of duty" for developmental purposes are being introduced into organizations, a subordinate still gets his best opportunity to learn from a superior who is willing to delegate and to nurture him in new undertakings.

Key behavioral cues for the Instructor are:

Understanding	Coaches
Encouraging	Listens
Educates	Trusting
Open	Candid
Guides	Nurtures
Trains	

DIPLOMAT (RC 0). The Diplomat sits on the fence between being a high achiever and a low achiever. He is sometimes one and sometimes the other. Basically relationship-centered, his dealings are with and about people. The difference between the Diplomat and the Instructor is that the Diplomat "uses" people rather than developing them. He is concerned more with self or organization than with the individual. He can be a high achiever as long as people don't catch on to his game, but once they sense they have been used, they react negatively and achievement falls.

His tightrope existence often turns the Diplomat into a compromiser who settles for less than the best solution in order to keep the greatest number of people happy. He is highly political, and very sensitive to the games people play, largely because he tends to be a consummate games-player himself. He is socially fluid, and believes that who you know is more important than what you know. The Diplomat needs to keep moving in order to remain effective, because eventually people recognize him for what he is and react negatively. He can cause very high levels of frustration by his refusal to be tied down to a strong and clear position. A common trait is that he is reluctant to make up his mind on issues, and is influenced by the last person to see him. This can be very upsetting if you happen to have been second to last.

Key behavioral cues for the Diplomat are:

Active	Joiner
Political	Manipulator
Mediator	Sociable
Polished	Compromiser
Agreeable	Visible

EMISSARY (RC −). The Emissary is a nonachiever. He is relationship-centered, but only in terms of his own needs. He deludes himself and others into thinking he is concerned about the organization, but his main goal is to be liked by everyone. He sees his role, therefore, as being the purveyor of good news. He thinks it is his duty to keep morale high. The organization should be a pleasant place to be, not necessarily to do work in. If there is a choice to be made between productivity and popularity, he will opt for the latter. His apparent motto is "People are everything," but what he really means is that his personal popularity is everything. The irony is that the Emissary sees himself as being effective, while others see him as being effective for a time, but change their opinions when they realize that the work never gets done.

Like the other negative styles, the Emissary is dominated by his own needs. His personality is one that craves stroking; he has to be liked by everyone. Everything else pales by comparison with this need. Unfortunately, he is unable to understand this and sometimes becomes a pitiable figure, making jokes and acting the hail-fellow-well-met character when it is most inappropriate. He is likable outside the job, but high achievers find him terribly annoying at work.

Key behavioral cues for the Emissary are:

Amusing	Cloying
Brotherly	Chummy
Harmony-oriented	Irresponsible
Optimistic	Weak
Indecisive	

MANAGERIAL ACHIEVEMENT VS. PERSONAL ACHIEVEMENT

In our discussion of the nine managerial styles of the M.ach One system, we have talked about achievement and have remarked that some of the styles are high-achievement styles, whereas others are low-achievement styles. But as you will recall, we have also said that achievement results from using the appropriate style *for the job*. If the job is part of the achievement equation, then how can we say that a management style brings about either high or low achievement without looking at the job itself?

The issue is whether a manager using a certain style is primarily concerned with *personal* achievement (that is, personal reward, personal satisfaction), or *managerial* achievement (achieving high levels of results in the critical areas of the job). In the M.ach One model, the three negative styles are exhibited by managers who are primarily concerned with *personal* achievement, whereas the three positive styles describe the behavior of managers who are concerned with *managerial* achievement. Although achievement may result from a negative style, it is unlikely unless the goals of the organization happen to coincide exactly with the goals of the individual. But since the basic aims of the Autocrat, Emissary, and Defector are to bully, to be loved, and to avoid responsibility, respectively, achievement, in an organizational sense, seems rather improbable.

Achievement is concerned not just with what *type* of basic behavior is used (TC, SC, or RC), but with *how* it is applied, that is, the managerial style used. For example, there is a world of difference between the following two applications of task-centered behavior (TC):

1. "We're running an hour behind schedule on this job, and it must get out by 5 o'clock or else we'll lose the order. John, you drop what you're doing and help Fred and Joe immediately. You can finish your own work with a little extra effort later. This job is really important to us, so please get started right away." (Benevolent Autocrat)

2. "Drop everything right now, John, and get onto the Higgins job immediately. And *hurry up*! We haven't got all bloody day!" (Autocrat)

These two statements have the same basic goal, but the second one reflects a personality that is insensitive to, and unconcerned about, the needs of the subordinate. The Autocrat is tied up with his *own* needs—to take out his frustration and anger on something or somebody, to assert authority, or to bully. The Benevolent Autocrat is able to communicate the urgency of the situation and give the appropriate order without getting personal or emotional; he is responsive to the requirements of the *job* rather than his own personal needs.

Broadly speaking, managers who exhibit the positive, high-achievement styles are *organization-centered*. They are concerned with achieving the organization's goals and needs in order to do a good job. Managers who exhibit the negative, low-achievement styles, tend to be more *self-centered*. They are primarily concerned with satisfying their own needs and goals, regardless of whether these coincide with those of the organization. As we have remarked, the Autocrat is concerned with satisfying his need for power, the Emissary his need for being liked, and the Defector his desire to beat the system. On the other end of the achievement scale, the Benevolent Autocrat is concerned with doing the job well, the Instructor with developing human resources, and the Professional with combining diverse resources to achieve specific goals.

Interestingly enough, what makes the Technocrat, Diplomat, and Bureaucrat neutral in terms of achievement is that these managerial styles all sit on the fence. Their goals may or may not coincide with those of the organization. Often the Technocrat uses technology for its own sake, simply because he gets a kick out of it, but there are also many Technocrats who are highly effective in the design of systems and the application of new technology. The same can be said for the Bureaucrat; sometimes he plays by the rule book just to be stubborn (hence the common use of *bureaucrat* as a highly derogatory term, often preceded by words unsuitable for print), but there are times when maintenance of clear rules and procedures is of vital importance for organizational success. We all use the style of the Diplomat now and then, using relationships with people to help ourselves achieve certain goals, and when these goals coincide with the organization's goals, the style can be highly effective.

In the light of these remarks, the style profiles, and the discussion of style and achievement, examine your scores on the Managing Style Location Test (Exercise 3-1) and evaluate yourself critically. Are there areas where you should be behaving differently in order to achieve more? Are there some things you should try to stop doing? Are there some other things you should try to do more often? Are there some styles that you aren't using enough, or others you are using far too much? Increasing your level of achievement as a manager means changing your behavior in some way. If you're serious about improving your management style you might as well start now to consider where changes need to be made.

Finally, when you've had a chance to think about your own behavior and its effects, look at the people with whom you work and how they behave. We will give you some advice on how to handle people with various difficult styles, but none of that will be of much use if you don't know what styles they're exhibiting. Try to identify the predominant styles of your boss, colleagues, and subordinates, and think of the most appropriate way of respondng to them. (It is *not* advisable to tell them they're Diplomats, Autocrats, Emissaries, and the like—they won't know what you're talking about.)

If you know someone who is, say, an Autocrat, and the style annoys you, you can perhaps screen out some of the emotional content in what that person says or does, and get on with the job without becoming emotional yourself. If you understand the behavior, it is considerably easier to deal with it.

4

Motivation: Keeping the Drive Alive

Vince Lombardi, the great former head coach of the Green Bay Packers, once said, "Winning isn't everything; it's the only thing." This philosophy is shared by a number of his colleagues in the sports world as well as by people in many other walks of life. The essence of Lombardi's statement is that you have to have a clear goal against which to measure your performance: either you win, or you lose. If you win, presumably you did your job well, and if you lose, you didn't do it well enough. Of course, the corollary to this is that when you win, you gain a tremendous feeling of satisfaction, a feeling that makes all the hours, days, weeks, and months of hard work, anguish, and anxiety well worth it. The sporting world knows the feeling well, but, as any manager can tell you, it is not only through sports that one experiences "the thrill of victory and the agony of defeat."

All behavior is goal-oriented. We do everything for a reason, even though it sometimes seems "unreasonable" in the eyes of others. Lombardi's goal was to win. But what that really meant was he wanted to perform his job better than anyone else. Because his occupation involved a game, many people who subscribed to the notion that "It's not whether you win or lose, it's how you play the game" found Lombardi's dedication to winning "unreasonable." Well, which is right? Do we have to "win" at everything? Isn't it enough simply to do our best? Or are there times when, because of other aspects of the "game," we shouldn't even go that far?

Not everyone is driven by the need to excel. There is a wide range of motivations, as every manager knows. Some people respond very well to certain treatment and incentives, whereas others remain unmoved. The question of motivation is complex, at best. We know that unless individuals are "motivated" to do something, their performances will be lackluster and no amount of training or experience will be of any help. The question is not so much whether individuals can do something (although all the desire in the world is useless unless one possesses a certain amount of knowledge and skill), but whether they *will* do it. Motivation is critical to managerial and organizational success.

WHAT IS MOTIVATION?

When we talk about motivation we are basically referring to the driving force that stimulates behavior and channels it in specific directions. The commercial that shows a little boy complaining about having to paint a fence and that ends up with him lying in a hammock, speckled with paint,

57

and saying "Energize me!" illustrates this issue superbly. Energy isn't what the little rascal lacks, nor is it motivation. He is highly motivated to play baseball, or football, or "aliens from outer space," and he can play with great vigor at these things from early morning to bedtime. What he doesn't have is the *specific* motivation—hence the "energy"—to paint the fence. Motivation, from a managerial or organizational viewpoint, is more than just "energizing" people. It means channeling their energy toward the accomplishment of the organization's goals. Everyone is motivated: it's just that some people don't appear to be motivated in the direction we'd like them to be.

Motivation is a complex process, but because it is essential to organizational success, managers should attempt to gain some understanding of it. Having a list of "things to do to motivate people" is not enough. It's not that simple, and this type of approach usually leads to great problems. The manager who starts to toy with basic human processes without knowing what he or she is doing can be spotted easily by everyone, and employees resent such unthinking "manipulation" tremendously. Therefore it is important to have some knowledge of the basic ideas about motivation that are now generally accepted by managers and teachers. The M.ach One approach to motivation is practical and applicable to working situations, and is supported by a great deal of research and testing.

Before you continue reading this chapter, you will find it useful to complete the Managerial Motivation Test in Exercise 4-1. Respond to it with your present job in mind. A scoring key appears at the end of the chapter, but you should finish reading the chapter before you score yourself on the exercise. Like the Managing Style Location Test, this test will provide you with some feedback on your style of management.

Exercise 4-1 Complete the Managerial Motivation Test

The Managerial Motivation Test is a measure of self-perceived motivational patterns. It is designed for use by managers to enable them to examine their motivational needs in relation to the jobs they presently occupy. Results should be used as a basis of discussion rather than as validated diagnostic findings.

INSTRUCTIONS

On the following page there are ten sets of statements which you are asked to consider. Look at the first set and decide the degree to which each of the three statements, (a), (b) and (c), describe how you feel about your job.

In the column headed "Weight," place a "5" beside the statement which you think describes your feelings best, a "3" beside the next most descriptive statement of your feelings, and a "1" beside the statement which seems to reflect your feelings towards your job least. Continue in this fashion through each of the remaining nine sets of statements.

Respond to *every* statement, making sure that you allocate a "5", "3", and "1" in each set. Do not give equal ratings to two statements in the same set—i.e., you can't give a "5" to both statement (a) and statement (b) in the same set. You must make a choice between weightings in every instance, even though you sometimes feel that all statements apply to you equally or that none describe your feelings adequately.

When you have responded to all ten statement sets, transfer your weightings to the Response Form below. Scoring and analysis keys will be provided later.

Managerial Motivation Test Response Form

	(a)	(b)	(c)
1.			
2.			
3.			
4.			
5.			
6.			
7.			
8.			
9.			
10.			

Managerial Motivation Test

		Weight
1	(a) I like to feel that I have control over the success or failure of any job I take on.	
	(b) I prefer to make group rather than individual decisions.	
	(c) I feel a responsibility for building my organization into a strong and effective one.	
2	(a) I enjoy working hard.	
	(b) I think that one of the most important aspects of any job is the personal friendships that develop from it.	
	(c) I believe that the most satisfying aspect of a job is a feeling of personal accomplishment.	
3	(a) I like to do each job better than the last one.	
	(b) I think that it is more important to achieve some of my organization's objectives than my own.	
	(c) I want to be liked by the people I work with.	
4	(a) I believe that it's important to take the time to listen carefully to subordinates' problems and to express sympathy and understanding.	
	(b) I like to see the tangible results of my actions, no matter whether they're good or poor.	
	(c) I think participative management is really a way to avoid responsibility.	
5	(a) I schedule my time and activities precisely and carefully.	
	(b) I believe that trust is a major part of any working relationship.	
	(c) I like to feel a challenge in any job I do.	
6	(a) I feel that people are what make an organization a good place to work.	
	(b) I prefer some formality in meetings I attend, with a chairperson and a clear agenda.	
	(c) I am willing to take calculated risks to accomplish something.	
7	(a) I try to establish clear and challenging goals for myself in my job.	
	(b) I enjoy socializing with colleagues off the job.	
	(c) There is little place for emotion in effective management.	

		Weight
8	(a) I don't feel comfortable in jobs which aren't clearly structured and defined.	
	(b) I actively seek out feedback about my job performance from my boss and others who work with me.	
	(c) I think an important part of my job is the development of subordinates.	
9	(a) I think that hard work and some personal sacrifice are the keys to success.	
	(b) I can't work well with people I don't like.	
	(c) I prefer to work independently of others.	
10	(a) An easy job is a boring job.	
	(b) To be an effective manager, I think you need strength and influence in your organization.	
	(c) I prefer a group approach to solving problems rather than trying to go it alone.	

THE MOTIVATION PROCESS

At its most basic, the motivation process involves: (1) needs or expectations, (2) behavior, (3) goals or objectives, and (4) feedback on performance. These aspects of motivation interact with one another, as shown in Figure 4-1.

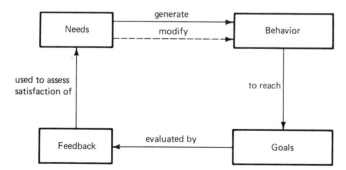

Figure 4-1. The Motivation Process

Motivation arises from some type of felt need. We experience a dis-equilibrium; we want or need something that we haven't got and as a result we experience a vague sense of being slightly out of balance. Often, of course, we are blissfully unaware of our own needs. We do certain things unquestioningly and the underlying needs being fulfilled are more apparent to others than they are to us. The basic assumption of all motivation theory, however, is that action is goal-oriented. We are "motivated" to achieve a goal, and, as Figure 4-1 illustrates, a need is felt, action is taken specifically directed toward fulfilling the need, the need level is modifed, and the cycle continues.

As the underlying need is fulfilled, it becomes less compelling. For instance, a starving person is solely motivated to acquire and consume food, but once the hunger is sated, the importance of food becomes less immediate. You can verify this reaction in another way. Offer a young child an ice cream cone if he or she will perform some simple job. The job will be performed willingly. Then offer another cone for another job (keep the jobs simple, but make sure they are not entertaining—you want to make the motivating factor the ice cream, not the job itself). Continue with another job, and then another, and soon the child will have had enough ice cream, and the jobs will have lost their attraction. The child will no longer be motivated to work because the underlying need has been satisfied. This example leads us to two important conclusions about motivation:

1. Behavior is both directed to, and results from unsatisfied needs.
2. Once a need is satisfied it is no longer a motivator.

The motivation process in general proceeds as illustrated in Figure 4-1. Individuals experience some need or disequilibrium; they believe that certain actions will reduce this felt need; the goal of their action becomes the reduction of the need; they receive feedback from a variety of sources as to how appropriate these actions have been in fulfilling the felt need; and finally, on the basis of this feedback, they modify their behavior, either intensifying or lessening the action, depending on how well it seems to be working. For example, an individual who feels insecure in his or her job will experience a need for security. The individual may decide that certain actions—for example, active participation in a union, securing written contracts of employment, becoming "indispensable," and so on—will make him or her more secure. The effects of these actions will then be monitored as to the degree of security they provide. Actions that make the individual feel secure will be maintained at what is felt to be an appropriate level; actions that don't will either be intensified, or else alternative actions will be tested. If the individual is given a contract of employment for life complete with financial guarantees, and if he or she accepts this as definite and permanent job security, the need for security will be extinguished and we can expect behavior to change, becoming directed to other unsatisfied needs.

BASIC MOTIVATIONAL DRIVES

If we accept the premise that unsatisfied needs are motivating factors and bring about behavior that is directed toward satisfying these needs, the next question a manager must ask is, what are these underlying needs? What motivates people? What do they want in their jobs? There appear to be some basic classes of needs that apply to the majority of people working in organizations. Focusing purely on behavior at work makes it somewhat easier to identify these basic needs because we are looking at a more limited range of relationships, roles, and activities.

One of the most widely accepted conceptions of motivational needs was developed by psychologist Abraham Maslow. Maslow's view of motivation has its basis in logic. It is the product of observation and of thought, and it is therefore attractive to managers, since they can see the phenomenon working in situations with which they are familiar. Taking Maslow's theory as a starting point, we can develop a model that fits the overall M.ach One system.

Maslow maintains that individuals are motivated to satisfy a number of needs, some of which are more powerful than others. We focus our attention and behavior on satisfying the most pressing needs first, and then move on to the less pressing ones. The process is a continual one—as one need becomes satisfied, and therefore less important to us, other needs loom up and become motivators of our behavior. This progression of needs is represented as a hierarchy or ladder (see Figure 4-2). The most immediate, most basic, most pressing needs are shown at the bottom of the ladder with other needs shown successively higher on the the ladder according to their

SELF-ACTUALIZATION
Reaching your maximum potential
Doing your thing best

ESTEEM
Respect from others.
Self-respect. Recognition.

BELONGING
Affiliation, acceptance,
being a part of something

SAFETY
Physical safety, psychological
security

PHYSIOLOGICAL
Hunger, thirst, sex, rest

Figure 4-2. The Basic Hierarchy of Needs

hierarchy of importance to the individual. Higher level needs do not become important until the lower level needs have been satisfied.

The primary needs of human beings are physiological ones—hunger, thirst, sex, and rest. When an individual lacks the basic elements of existence, these needs will totally obsess thought and behavior. Once these first-level physiological needs are satisfied, individuals become concerned with the need for safety and security—protection from physical harm, disaster, and illness, and security of family, income, lifestyle, and relationships. In other words, once our stomachs are full, we begin to think about how we can keep them that way.

Human beings have the first two levels of needs in common with all other animals, but in addition we have another powerful and basic need, the need to belong. Donne's statement that "No man is an island unto himself" is most profound because it reflects the universal truth that all human beings, except for the rare individual, must live and work within a framework of relationships. We are gregarious animals and we all have a fundamental need to feel that we belong somewhere and to some group, be it family, friends, association, club, or whatever. We need to feel accepted by others and to be the recipients of some loyalty and trust.

Some Western organizations do a good job of making their employees feel a strong bond of affiliation and loyalty. They are able to make their members feel part of a group that values, supports, and protects them. But this type of organization is rare in our Western culture. Most North American and European organizations generally have a highly tenuous bond with their employees. We pay them a salary and give them benefits and usually try to provide a certain degree of job security, but more often than not employees are left to establish their strong ties outside their work.

The Japanese, who seem to be incredibly successful at inspiring loyalty, take a different approach. Employees are made to feel a strong sense of belonging to the organization. For example every employee of Matsushita recites the code of values and sings the company song with his fellow workers at the start of every workday. They state their loyalty, *and the company reciprocates.* Matsushita does not fire people. It stands by its employees and offers them the loyalty and support it expects to receive from them. There is no sense of unrequited love here. As in most of the large Japanese organizations, employees are made to feel part of a "family," and their social life is largely centered around their "relatives" in the company. They rarely leave the organization to work for another one because this would mean not only leaving their friends and "family," but actually becoming regarded as a "traitor" by members of *both* organizations. A Japanese manager who at age forty leaves his company for a job elsewhere can expect to take a 40 percent cut in salary.

Does this type of attention fulfill the need to belong and motivate employees to higher performance? Although it's not the only contributing factor by any means, organizations that do inspire a sense of belonging show some remarkable statistics. For one, their employees are deeply committed to helping "their" organization perform better. In 1979, for example, Toyota received 527,000 employee suggestions for improvements. The average was about 12 suggestions per employee. At Matsushita in the same year, the company received about 25 suggestions per employee. That these were not just idle comments is demonstrated by the fact that 85–90 percent of the suggestions were implemented by management! Now *that's* a feeling of belonging!

The need to feel a part of something is closely related to, and in fact actually evolves into, a need for *esteem,* that is, a need to feel a sense of self-worth. The need for esteem has two components. First is the need to be respected by others, to be given recognition and praise, and secondly, the need to feel good about oneself, to feel that you are contributing something worthwhile, that you are a valued member of society, that you are proud of yourself and think you're a decent person. This is a critical factor in everyone's life; we need to feel that we have some substance, some direction, some worth. When these feelings are absent, individuals drift aimlessly, experience deep confusion and depression, and see no point to their lives. We all know how important a feeling of esteem is to ourselves, but as managers, do we consider how our employees feel about themselves, their lives, and their jobs? The comments of an automobile worker in Studs Terkel's marvellous book *Working* make the point:

> You really begin to wonder. What price do they put on me? Look at the price they put on the machine. If that machine breaks down, there's somebody out there to fix it right away. If I break down, I'm pushed over to the other side until another man takes my place. The only thing they have on their mind is to keep that line running.

Finally, Maslow says, when all these needs have been satisfied, people are motivated, at least to some extent, by a desire for *self-actualization,* to achieve whatever they define as their maximum potential, to do their work to the best of their ability. This concept is rather too vague to be of much use to a practicing manager. How do you motivate an individual by self-actualization? How do you even know what that means? Does it mean that you motivate people by letting them do whatever they want, or can we be a bit more specific? Fortunately, we can and will be much more specific about what motivates people, but first we should note some important points that Maslow's approach brings out.

As Maslow observes, individuals do *not* experience only one need at a time. Maslow argues, and all the research supports the contention, that we probably experience a wide variety of needs all the time, but only to varying degrees. It could be said that hunger is not a problem in North America, yet we have all experienced the phenomenon of not being able to concentrate on a job because of a growling stomach. Productivity drops just prior to lunch as people transfer their thoughts from their jobs to the upcoming meal.

After lunch, food is not uppermost in most people's minds, but perhaps rest is, as a feeling of drowsiness may set in.

Similarly, in almost all organizational settings, individuals juggle their need for *security* ("Can I keep this job?") with the need for *esteem* ("If I do what is required in the job, how will my peers see me, and how will I see myself?"). In a situation where management demands a certain level of performance, but group norms are to produce below these levels, all these issues are experienced. If the individual does not produce at the level demanded by management, he may lose his job (security). But if he conforms to management's norms rather than to those of his group, he may be ostracized (belonging) and regarded as a turncoat (esteem), and he may see himself as having let the team down (self-esteem). We don't progress from one level in the hierarchy of needs to another in a straightforward, orderly manner; there is a constant but ever-changing pull from all levels and all types of needs.

Although not everyone experiences the needs suggested by Maslow in the order he places them, in general physical, social and individual needs motivate us to certain behavior. Organizations tend to overlook the fact that satisfied needs no longer act as motivators. Most incentive systems are based on needs that have already been largely satisfied. If management placed emphasis on needs that have *not* been satisfied, rather than on those that have been relatively well taken care of, employees would more likely be motivated toward achieving the goals of the organization. It must be borne in mind that human behavior is directed primarily toward *unsatisfied* needs. If the pay is good and the job is secure, then more pay and more security don't do much. On the other hand, if the job is not secure and the pay is poor, then job enrichment, quality circles, worker participation, and so on aren't of much use. You have to have the basic needs satisfied first, and once you do, you need to move on to higher levels of motivators.

MOTIVATION AND THE M.ACH ONE SYSTEM

One of the problems managers encounter when they read about motivation, communication, leadership, or decision-making is that despite the considerable research and available information in each of these areas, each topic is treated separately, as though there were no clear or systematic relationship between them. No manager is naive enough to think that all his or her problems are "communication problems," or "motivation problems," or whatever. Successful managing involves integrated, coordinated, and consistent behavior in all these areas. You have to get the message across to your people, you have to turn them on, you have to lead them, and you have to make decisions concerning them, with them. And you must be consistent in the way you do all this. If there is one trait that subordinates fear and dislike more than anything in a boss, it's inconsistency. We can endure many hardships, but when we don't know from day to day or hour to hour whether we'll be treated well, poorly, or indifferently, we become very upset. Although it is somewhat removed from a managerial situation, the experience of the U.S. prisoners in Iran illustrates this reaction. They could cope with the idea of being shot, imprisoned, or isolated, but they had great difficulty coping with the irregular, irrational, unpredictable changes in moods of their captors. They never knew what to expect. We all need some degree of certainty in our lives; that's simply a basic human characteristic.

M.ach One links motivation to the other major dimensions of managing by focusing on the three most important motivational needs in an organizational setting: the need for achievement, the need for power, and the need for affiliation. These three basic needs tend to manifest themselves in behavior that is either task-centered, situation-centered, or relationship-centered.

The Need for Achievement

The *single* motivating factor that has received the most attention in research is the need for achievement. The need for achievement is the basic need to do things better than you have done them before—to achieve some performance goal. The manager who spends his or her time thinking about doing a better job, achieving some outstanding goal, or doing something really important has a high need for achievement (abbreviated as n-ach).

High achievers abound in our society. Their behavior, both at work and outside it, is focused on meeting challenges. These people are successful entrepreneurs and effective managers in dynamic and challenging organizations. Studies of individuals who possess a high need for achievement have identified a number of their common characteristics.

First, the high achiever likes situations and jobs in which he or she takes personal responsibility for solving problems and for the outcomes of his or her actions. If the actions of others determine the outcome of a situation and you have little to do with it, you obviously won't derive the same satisfaction as you would from doing it all yourself. At least, that's how the high n-ach individual reasons. By the same token, the high n-ach person is not a gambler; he or she prefers to "win" through personal effort and intelligence rather than by chance. As a result, we don't usually find high achievers in situations where outside influences have a major effect on outcomes. The high n-ach manager exudes self-confidence. He believes he can do a job well if given the responsibility, and he usually can, simply because he's more concerned and has probably spent more time thinking about how to do it than someone with less drive for achievement.

Secondly, individuals with high n-ach set *moderate* goals for themselves. They avoid setting goals that are either unrealistically high (and therefore most likely unattainable) or so low that achieving them brings little or no satisfaction. There is no satisfaction in failure, and none in doing what is too easy. The most satisfying challenge is one that stretches you to your utmost, but that by dint of energy, skill, and intelligence you conquer. Interestingly enough, for some people this characteristic can be identified at an early age, as shown by psychologists in experiments with small children who are first invited for an interview on some pretext, then left alone while the psychologist is "called away" for a few minutes. The children are asked to amuse themselves by playing a game while the experimenter is out of the room, and a set of beanbags and a wastebasket are produced. The game is simply to throw the beanbags into the basket. Without any further comment or instructions, the psychologist leaves the office and moves to the other side of a one-way mirror to observe the children. Those with a high need for achievement have one characteristic in common as they play the game: they adjust their distance from the basket so that they neither get all the beanbags in, nor do they get only a few in the basket. In other words, they move forward or backward until they find the distance at which it is challenging to throw bags into the basket. If they get all the bags in, the task is too easy, and if they get none or a very few in, it is too difficult. The goal of the high achiever is to make the game moderately difficult, but "winnable" with effort, energy, and skill. On the other hand, children who have low need for achievement either tend not to engage in the game, or else stand at random distances and miss all their throws, or dump all the bags in the basket at once.

A third characteristic of high n-ach individuals is that they prefer to take calculated risks. They enjoy situations in which there is a chance of failure but the risk is not so great that it cannot be overcome by their own energy, skill, and intelligence. Successful managers who constantly complain about "problems" and whose life is beset by overwork are often the very creators of all these problems and work. The fact is that they love it, and "complaining" about it merely affords them an opportunity to talk about all the things they revel in.

The final major characteristic of the high n-ach individual is the desire for rapid, constant, and concrete feedback on performance. The high achiever has to know how he or she is doing! The reason is twofold. First, how else can you obtain satisfaction from your accomplishments? And secondly, if you don't know how you're doing, how can you ever improve? To the high achiever it is just as important to find out that he or she is doing badly as it is to know that things are going well. This is not to say that doing badly is satisfying, but if your goal is to do well, then you have to know when you're getting off track so that you can make the necessary adjustments—and the sooner you know the better.

The Need for Power

In an organizational sense, the need for power (abbreviated as n-pow) is the basic need to manage the behavior of others in order to achieve the organization's goals. N-pow does not necessarily imply a need for autocratic, tyrannical behavior, but rather a need to have some impact, to be influential and effective in achieving organizational goals. If an individual spends his or her time thinking about how to influence and control the behavior of others, how to win arguments, how to change other people's behavior and maintain authority over their actions, he or she is exhibiting a need for power.

The high n-pow individual has certain obvious characteristics, one of which is the tendency to try to influence others directly by initiating suggestions, giving opinions, arguing certain points of view, and generally trying to convince others to follow certain courses of action. High n-pows are often articulate, talkative, and persuasive.

The major difference between a high n-ach manager and a high n-pow manager is that the latter is much more *organization minded.* He or she tends to feel a greater degree of responsibility for building and sustaining the organization to which he belongs and will subordinate individual goals to corporate goals. The high n-pow manager believes in more centralized authority, probably because he or she knows how hard it is to implement decisions, especially in large organizations. Satisfaction of the need for power is far removed from banging the fist on the table and issuing orders; the successful n-pow manager knows that his major task is the persistent cajoling, prodding, stroking, threatening, dealing, and coaxing required to get things done. Such are the realities of organizational life. At higher levels, things can only be done by and through others, and the individual with a very high need for achievement, with all its implications for going it alone and taking individual responsibility, is less likely to succeed. One has to become more organization-minded and less individual minded.

Another interesting characteristic of the manager with a high need for power is that he or she likes to work. Although the achievement-oriented individual tries to minimize work while maximizing results, the power-oriented manager actually enjoys hard work for its own sake. There is a certain amount of satisfaction to be gained from hard work, and given the process of constant persuasion and "politicking" needed in many jobs, the n-pow manager must be prepared to spend long hours wooing and pressuring the various individuals and groups that can help accomplish desired goals.

The high n-pow manager is an "organization man" and is willing to sacrifice a great deal of self-interest for the good of the organization. Because of the "political" aspects of influencing a number of other people to focus their actions in a certain way, and the heavy commitment of time and energy this requires, the high n-pow manager has to invest a large portion of himself and his life in "the organization." This is not the case with the high n-ach individual, whose concern is to do things himself and to avoid, as much as possible, the net of interdependencies and political maneuvering in the organization. The n-pow manager believes that hard work and sacrifice should, and will, be rewarded.

A high need for power as a motivational drive is most useful and effective in positions at or near the top of organizations, or in project management. It becomes difficult to "go it alone" at the top of a large organization or at the head of a project group. The need for achievement, with its connotations of individual effort and concern, must give way to a need that can be satisfied by achieving certain goals and objectives through the actions of other people. Research indicates that the heads of organizations who have a high need for power and whose subordinates have a high need for achievement tend to be highly successful.

The Need for Affiliation

The need for affiliation is the need to belong, to be liked by others, to be held in some esteem. Individuals who enjoy helping others, who are concerned with the growth and development of subordinates, who are fond of spending time in lengthy "bull sessions," and who are good listeners tend to have a high need for affiliation (n-affil).

High n-affil individuals like to be part of a group. They prefer to share in accomplishments rather than to take individual initiative and sole responsibility. They are often presented with opportunities to capitalize on and take credit for ideas and actions that they conceived and initiated, but they generally do not have a high need for recognition for individual achievement and are usually quite happy to have their group or department receive the credit. They prefer participation, group effort, and consensus decisions. The high n-affil individual values relationships over accomplishments and friendship over power. Harmony, respect, and affection are much more important sources of satisfaction than results and accomplishments. Although these are not the major criteria for success in many jobs, most managerial positions require a certain amount of sensitivity toward people, and most of us have some need for affiliation.

Individuals with a combination of a high need for affiliation and a low need for achievement tend to be unsuccessful in managerial positions. Their subordinates tend to view them as poor bosses who are too easily swayed by immediate pressures. In an effort to be fair to everyone, such individuals end up being inequitable, giving some things to some people and not to others simply because some individuals are more vocal and willing to make more of a fuss.

For the high n-affil manager, effectiveness largely depends on the job he or she occupies. This type of manager is invaluable in positions where development, support, and nurturance of subordinates are important. Training, managing creative people, or working with people who are making major transitions in life and jobs are activities in which high n-affil individuals can be very effective.

LINKING STYLE, MOTIVATION, AND THE JOB

The needs for achievement, power, and affiliation are the broad underlying sources of motivation for individuals in organizations. These drives encompass all the needs postulated by Maslow and are more specifically focused on the work situation. Apart from the basic physiological needs, achievement, power, or affiliation encompass the need for security, belonging, respect, and esteem. For instance, esteem can be generated by one's individual accomplishments, by one's power, status, and authority, or by the affection and friendship of one's peers. And even the vague and undefined need for self-actualization can be satisfied by reaching some pinnacle in any of these areas.

The problem with motivation is that we can't *see* it, we can only *infer* it from behavior. But we know that motivation is what makes people act, and since action is what we want in organizations, we need to know the major motivational drives of the people who work for and with us (and, of course, it would be helpful to know the same things about ourselves). It is impractical to have everybody fill out tests that measure their motivational set; in any case, motivational needs change over time. So how can we discover what makes people in our organizations tick?

Research shows that there is a strong link between an individual's underlying motivational set and his or her basic style of behavior. Individuals with a high need for achievement tend to exhibit task-centered behavior; those with a need for power tend to exhibit situation-centered behavior; and those who are motivated by a need for affiliation tend to exhibit relationship-centered behavior. These various management styles can be seen as reflections of underlying motivational needs. Therefore, if we can identify an individual's basic style of behavior, we may be able to determine what needs motivate him or her.

It is important to recognize that the *job* provides the "food" for motivation. If a job allows a high achiever to seek challenges, take personal responsibility, set goals, take calculated risks, and receive concrete feedback on performance, then that individual is going to be stimulated. Given the necessary skills, we can expect this person to be highly productive. By the same token, an individual who is motivated by a need for power should be placed in a job where he or she can exercise this desire, can influence others, can persuade them and lead them in the attainment of organizational goals. Placing a high n-pow individual in a specialized staff advisory position is not likely to produce great results. The staff advisor has, by definition, *no* power. His job is to advise others who, in turn, decide whether to implement or not. Frustrating a major motivational drive leads to unhappiness and poor performance.

M.ach One makes a *direct link* between management style, motivation, and the job. If we can identify an individual's basic style, we can infer his or her underlying motivational set, and then we can make sure that he or she is placed in a job that contains the appropriate motivational elements. The result is an individual doing what he or she does best, in a place where that behavior is required, and where he or she is likely to be rewarded for doing the right thing. We tend to like doing things that we do well, and, of course, we do them well because we like them. When we are *rewarded* for performing well, it's even better still. What a lovely self-reinforcing cycle!

Motivation leads to *behavior*, which, when applied in the appropriate *situation*, leads to *achievement*, which leads to *reward*, which leads to further *motivation*, and so on (see Figure 4-3).

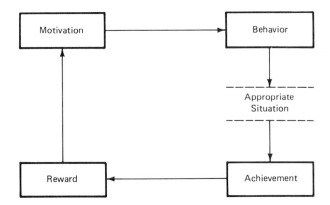

Figure 4-3.   The Link Between Motivation, Style, and the Job

The motivational aspect of work comes from matching the basic style of behavior to the job. It is *not* an external force, a gimmick that is "applied" to people. It is an intrinsic part of the job. When the job allows an individual to do what he or she does best (and therefore likes best), and rewards them for doing it, motivation results.

We can now see some of the reasons for Vince Lombardi's success. Lombardi was able to take people with certain abilities, put them in positions where they performed well (and therefore where they liked to be), and gave them the ultimate reward: "the thrill of victory." He stressed the idea of motivation—wanting to do well—and by placing his people in positions where they *could* do well, he got the most out of them.

The match between behavior, motivation, and job is the key to high achievement. It is simple, yet powerful. It explains why some people never achieve to their full potential, and why some people may be highly successful in one job yet fail in another. Somewhere there is a mismatch between the requirements of the job, the things that motivate the individual, and the behavior he or she is most comfortable with and can do best. As we know, individuals with a drive to achieve like to take on a challenge, get on with the job themselves, and receive frequent feedback on their performance. They are obviously successful in jobs that allow them to do these things. Take the example of a young engineer who has had a specific area of responsibility delegated to him and whose job has been challenging, essentially individual in nature, and has provided clear and measurable outputs. Likely to be a success, you say, and of course, you're right. But promote this bright, energetic, and successful engineer to a managerial job requiring more coordination, planning, and administration, and suddenly things change. Success now depends on the activities of many other people; there is a much wider range of measures that can be applied against performance, from financial data to efficiency figures to output totals; and the job is too wide to be done by one person alone. How does our bright young engineer cope with that? If the temptation to do what he likes best—that is, getting personally involved, working independently, "getting his fingers right in the grease"—is not resisted, we have a problem. The job can't be done with the individual's main management style, and it doesn't provide the factors that make it motivating. Unless there are some changes, either in underlying motivational drives or behavior, the individual may consistently do the wrong thing, be criticized for it, and therefore become more and more unhappy and achieve less and less. The person is the same—he is just as skilled and energetic as before—but the job doesn't provide an opportunity to do what that individual likes to do best, does best, and finds most motivating.

READING YOUR PEOPLE

To get the most out of people, to get them to achieve at their highest potential, we have to understand what motivates them. You can't *make* people perform to the best of their ability and energy. Close supervision, driving, goading, and pushing can get people to do enough, perhaps, to keep you off their backs, but the drive and the will to win that Vince Lombardi talked about, and that every successful leader knows about, is something that comes from *within* the individual. What has to be remembered above all is that we all have these drives in us already. The manager's job is to set up the situation so that we respond to it willingly with everything we've got. *That's* motivation.

A problem for every manager, however, is how to recognize the things that motivate each of the quite different people he or she may have as subordinates. You can't go around having people fill in tests every week. But you need to know what is likely to stimulate each subordinate. That's why we have looked at management style so closely. If you can recognize the predominant *style* of an individual, you can begin to sense his or her underlying motivational drives. It isn't a precise method, by any means, but it's much better than relying on sheer intuition. Often we place people in jobs simply because, like Everest, they're there. If you want high achievement, that's not the right approach. Make the job fit the person's style and motivation.

Of course, everything that has been said applies to you, too. If you want to achieve your best, then take a critical look at your style, at your motivational set, and at your job, and see how they match. Some adjustments may have to be made for the sake of a better alignment. We will be talking about some approaches to doing that in Chapter 7. Exercise 4-2, which follows, provides you with a chance to look at one of these elements —your motivational set.

Exercise 4-2. Score and analyze your Managerial Motivation Test

STEP 1: Take the numbers you wrote in the Response Form and transfer them to the MMT Scoring Blank. Starting with item 1, place the three numbers, in the same order as you have written them in the Response Form, in the spaces shown for item 1 on the Scoring Blank.

STEP 2: Proceed to item 2, and do the same thing. Note that the three numbers on your Response Form for item 2 will still be transferred onto the Scoring Blank in order, but they must be placed in the spaces indicated. This is most important.

Complete the transfer of scores for all ten items, making sure you place the numbers in the appropriate spaces, using the same order, left to right, as in the Response Form.

STEP 3: Total each COLUMN of the Scoring Blank.

STEP 4: Add total of Cols. 1, 4 and 7 to obtain your Need for Achievement score.

Add totals of Cols. 2 and 5 to obtain your Need for Affiliation score.

Add totals of Cols. 3 and 6 to obtain your Need for Power score.

STEP 5: Capsule descriptions of these basic motivational needs are given at the end of the exercise. Your scores simply indicate the *relative* strength of these needs as you see them in your job. The highest score points towards the basic motivational need which underlies most of your managerial actions.

MMT Scoring Blank

	Col. 1	Col. 2	Col. 3	Col. 4	Col. 5	Col. 6	Col. 7
1.	___	___	___				
2.			___		___		___
3.	___		___		___		
4.		___		___		___	
5.			___		___		___
6.			___	___	___		
7.	___	___	___				
8.		___	___	___			
9.			___		___		___
10.	___		___		___		
Totals:	___	___	___	___	___	___	___

add total Col. 1 _____   add total Col. 2 _____   add total Col. 3 _____

 + total Col. 4 _____   + total Col. 5 _____   + total Col. 6 _____

 + total Col. 7 _____   = n-affil score _____   = n-pow score _____

 = n-ach score _____

Need for achievement is the basic need to do things better than you've done them before, to achieve some goal of performance. Goals which result in a feeling of achievement are generally moderately difficult to attain. The high achiever is concerned with getting rapid and clear feedback on performance, is eager to accept a moderate challenge or risk, prefers to have control over the outcome of his or her actions and to be held responsible for them.

Need for affiliation is the need to belong. The high affiliate likes to be liked by others above all else, and to feel wanted as a member of a group. He or she prefers to work in a group setting rather than alone, prefers group decisions to having to make individual decisions, likes the idea of teamwork, tends to be a good listener, and is highly people-oriented. As a manager, he or she is usually interested in the growth and development of subordinates.

Need for power is the basic need to manage the behavior of others to achieve the organization's goals. The power-oriented individual prefers centralized authority, is more organizationally-centered than individually-centered (i.e. is more of an "organization man"), believes in hard work, and believes that this hard work will be rewarded in the long run. He or she is often concerned with creating good systems which regulate and coordinate behavior.

5

Decisions,
Decisions,
Decisions!

Decision-making is a fundamental managerial activity: everything depends on *what* decisions are made and *how* they are made. We often call effective managers "good decision-makers," but what does that mean? Does it mean they make the *right* decisions, that they make the most *acceptable* decisions, that they make the *quickest* decisions, or simply that they make the *most* decisions? By definition, decision-making always involves a choice among various ways of doing or accomplishing something. Because business can't go ahead without these choices being made, the process is a highly visible one.

But decisions vary. Some are trivial and how they are made doesn't really matter, whereas others are critical and cause major changes. It may not make much difference in the scheme of things if you wear one suit of clothes or another to work, if you lunch at one time versus another, or if you call a meeting in the morning or in the afternoon. On the other hand, decisions concerning what goods will be shipped from a plant, how work overloads will be handled in the office, when a new product will be launched, or when and how capital will be raised are important.

Two sets of factors determine whether something is trivial or important:

1. Our *personal* set of values, attitudes, needs, and goals (the things that make up what we call personality).

2. *Organizational* goals and objectives.

All decisions are made relative to some set of goals or desired results; we judge a decision on the basis of its contribution to, or attempted contribution to, some goal.

As in previous chapters, we suggest that you first complete a short exercise to see how you make decisions. Exercise 5-1 contains the Decision Style Inventory and instructions. Take the time to do it now, then read through the chapter, and, finally, score it using the key provided at the end of the chapter. Once again, this inventory is for your eyes only. It provides useful information about how you operate as a manager and is one more piece of information forming the basis of what you need to know to increase your level of achievement.

Exercise 5-1.   Complete the Decision Style Inventory

Five managerial situations, each requiring a decision, are described below. Please read each one, and then decide *how* you would make the decision in each case.

Note that you are *not* being asked *what* decision should be made, but rather *how* it should be made. In other words, you are asked to choose between three basic "styles" of decision-making:

- **The Command Style,** where you alone make the decision, based on your knowledge of the situation.

- **The Consultation Style,** where you solicit the opinions of others concerned, but reserve the right to make the final decision yourself.

- **The Consensus Style,** where you gather the people concerned with the decision together and get them to come to a consensus.

You might wish to make a few brief notes to remind yourself of why you chose one particular decision-making style over another in each situation.

Situation 1

Your firm has just developed a new product that will hopefully make a major contribution to corporate profits. Because of declining markets for its existing products, the company is depending on this new line to provide both growth and profits, although the situation is not yet critical.

You are responsible for the pricing of the product and realize that if it is priced too low, increased sales will simply magnify losses, while if it is too high, sales will be inadequate to cover overheads. You have in front of you a complete set of financial projections and the company's balance sheet and profit and loss statement.

What style should you adopt in making the pricing decision?

Situation 2

Your company manufactures microcircuitry for electronic instruments, using a system which employs an etching process and molten copper in place of standard wiring to link components. It is an advanced technology, and the people in your group are highly skilled experts. You are a research scientist in charge of circuit development, and one of the few people with the knowledge and experience necessary for the job. You supervise ten bright but less experienced researchers. Their creativity and drive never cease to amaze you.

The team has developed a new alloy apparently superior to copper, and although it has not been tested extensively, it has passed most required standards. You have just received a request to make a recommendation on the new process to prospective buyers who will arrive tomorrow morning. You note that the time is now 6:00 p.m.

What decision style should you adopt in this situation?

Situation 3

You are the manager of the woods operation for a medium-sized pulp and paper company. You are attempting to decide whether to change the compensation program for loggers who cut the pulp wood. At present they are paid on an hourly basis, but you are thinking of implementing an incentive system based on group production. The company currently supplies all equipment such as chain saws, hard hats, gloves, etc. Under the proposed new system, the men would be responsible for buying and maintaining their own equipment.

What decision style should you adopt in this situation?

Situation 4

Recently it has come to your attention, as Distribution Manager of a local beverage company, that your shipper has been making informal deals with the firm's sales representatives whereby both parties have gained financially. This practice, while not specifically forbidden by company rules, has aspects which make it undesirable in your opinion. Upon investigation you have discovered that the practice is relatively widespread among the sales representatives, and that the amounts of money involved are growing. You feel you should take some action.

What decision style should you adopt in this situation?

Situation 5

You are the manager of a department containing thirty women who operate weaving looms for a textile firm. Although the looms are automated, the operators are very important because they have to watch the material carefully to detect flaws, and if they fail to do so, hundreds of feet of material may be ruined. If, for instance, a single strand of incorrectly dyed thread is woven into material of another color, the entire batch may have to be either scrapped or sold at a significantly reduced price. Some errors are unavoidable, and the women operating the looms are allowed a certain number of feet of wastage per week. However, if they exceed this allotted amount, financial penalties are levied against them.

The employees in this department have all been there for fifteen years or more, and some have been with the company for in excess of twenty years. You have known all the women involved in the department for a long time, and relationships are friendly and informal. You see some of them occasionally in various social settings, and a number of them have come to you with personal problems which you have helped them with.

A new type of loom is currently being tested in the department, and it seems clear that it is able to produce a higher quality of material, at a much higher production rate. Unfortunately, the loom is more difficult to operate than the ones presently in use. You have decided to buy ten of the new looms, and must now decide which women to train as operators. The training period is only two weeks long, and experience as an operator will be a great advantage.

What decision style should you adopt in this situation?

INFORMATION AND DECISION-MAKING

The basis of all decision-making is information. Without the right information and without adequate information, high-quality decisions cannot be made. We live in a time characterized by an information explosion—the amount of data available to us is overwhelming, and increasing daily at an incredible rate. Managers commonly complain that they get *too much* information. One manager is known to receive a stack of computer printouts each morning that he claims would take him three to four hours to scrutinize. He regularly looks at only one or two percent of the data provided, and now and then at another four or five percent. The time and effort involved in redesigning the type and format of information presented to him would take him several weeks and a great deal of arguing, so he simply stacks the material in a corner of his office and has it removed every weekend by the garbage collectors. It's clearly as frustrating to get too much information as it is to get too little.

Making a good decision is not simply a function of having a certain amount of information; it's more a matter of having the right type of information. The crash of 1929 caused problems for American industry, including the great General Motors. Alfred Sloan, the founder and head of GM as we know it, was concerned with how best to cope with the cataclysmic events of the time. Sales at GM had gone from $1.5 billion in 1929 to $983 million in 1930 — a drop of some $67 million, or 45 percent! But Sloan didn't simply start cutting and slashing the organization to decrease costs. Nor did he make any precipitous decisions. Instead, he addressed a letter to the members of the operations committee, which was made up of the top executives in the corporation, asking that they examine the situation closely from their own particular viewpoints, try to identify areas of weakness in GM, and make recommendations to overcome them. This letter of January 9, 1931, is recorded in Sloan's book *My Years at General Motors.* In part, it reads,

> I want to say that one of the principal points of business at the next meeting will be a contribution from each member as to what in his opinion have constituted weaknesses in procedure, policy or thought in the year just closed that should be eliminated and what new points can be developed that will be helpful in the year 1931.

How to react to the catastrophic events of the crash of 1929 was not the decision of one man at General Motors. Sloan knew that what was needed was information from a *variety of sources*, that analysis of the problem had to take into account the specific viewpoints and problems of *each part* of the organization, and that the firm's operating committee *as a group* would be able to decide what facts or opinions were relevant to the decisions that had to be made. He controlled the flow of information by limiting it to the contributions of the operating committee members, rather than soliciting opinions from managers in the corporation at large, and he ensured its relevance by insisting that each committee member support his own opinions with hard data. The information generated in these meetings was therefore designed to be appropriate both in terms of quantity and quality.

But information can be mismanaged, too. The mere gathering of data does not guarantee that a good decision will result, as illustrated by the Ford Motor Company's decision to produce the Edsel. Ford was not, and is not, a naive, seat-of-the-pants company. The Edsel decision began in 1948 with Henry Ford II's proposal to the executive committee that the company should look into the introduction of a brand new design of medium-priced car. In 1955, after a great deal of thought and study, the decision to design and manufacture a new car was made, and in 1957 the Edsel was introduced.

The information base for the Edsel decision was immense. It began with a six-volume study predicting major changes in the U.S. economy over the next ten years. It was followed by thousands of hours of design work to create a model that was different—but not too different—from any other North American automobile. Exhaustive studies were done to determine the psychological profiles of car buyers, and to establish the ''personality'' that the new car should portray. Thousands of names were reviewed. The poet Marianne Moore was retained to make suggestions, and the New York advertising agency Foote, Cone & Belding generated eighteen thousand names.

Despite the mass of information that had been gathered, or maybe because of it, time began to run short, and a number of the critical decisions had to be made in a rush, with little regard for the accumulated data. The original economic data in 1955 clearly supported the introduction of a new medium-sized car, but two years later the whole scene had changed. In addition, eighteen thousand names were obviously too great a number to handle, and in the end the name Edsel was chosen by the chairman of the board (it had not even been on the list of final choices). And since the data gathered on the ''personality profile'' for a new car were too complex to be of much use, the Edsel's design was influenced more by production deadlines than anything else. Ford did its homework—it gathered all the information it could possibly need, yet it still made a decision that cost the company some $350 million. One of the lessons of this experience is that information has to be relevant, manageable, and timely. At Ford in 1955, it wasn't.

Information forms the basis of all decisions. To a large extent, the effectiveness of a decision depends on the quantity, quality, and type of information gathered. We want neither too much nor too little; we want the right amount and the right type. Easier said than done, perhaps, but nevertheless true.

MAJOR ELEMENTS IN DECISION-MAKING

The general comments made so far have raised a number of important points about decisions that we will now examine in more detail. They include the following:

- Relative importance and consequences
- Information base
- Personal values
- Individual vs. group decision-making
- Quality of the decision
- Acceptance of the decision
- Time constraints

Relative Importance and Consequences

All decisions have to be scrutinized and evaluated as to their relative importance. This is the issue raised in the first two chapters of this book—setting priorities. Decisions are action points, and actions take time and energy. Given the limited amount of both time and energy, it is essential that a manager evaluate the types and number of decisions he or she has to make and assign them priorities. Some decisions are routine and do not involve analyzing new and complex data or coming up with a unique judgment. Such decisions can be made quickly and require little new information; you simply check the few important facts that determine whether you will take one action versus some other, and the rules say that a certain decision will be made. When to lay off employees, when to hire temporary help, when to use overtime, and so on, are matters that are usually clearly laid out by organizational procedures. Guidelines exist and action is taken on that basis. By the same token, requests for expenditures may be ratified almost automatically if they fall within budgetary limits, and purchasing of materials and supplies may be governed more by formula and procedure than by individual analysis and decisions.

Many managers, however, find themselves bogged down with trivial and essentially routine decisions. The fault may lie with the system or with the individual. Every manager should take some time to list the various *types* of decisions that he or she makes in the job. Which are administrative, production-oriented, personnel, financial, and so on? Your own categories will no doubt be more specific than these.

Secondly, managers should examine these categories of decisions and ask three questions about them:

1. How important is each decision to the successful completion of my job and to the effectiveness of the organization?
2. Who should best make or be involved in each of these decisions?
3. What type of information is necessary for each of these decisions?

The responses to these questions indicate the priorities, degree of delegation, and structure required to handle the decisions in a job. The more important the decision, the more likely it is that the manager will retain control over it, and the more complex the information needed to make it. These relationships are shown in Figure 5-1.

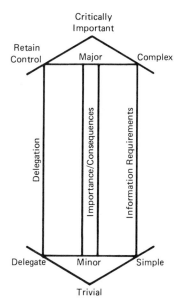

Figure 5-1. The Relationship between the Relative Importance of a Decision and the Structure Needed to Handle It Effectively

Information Base

Although the basis of all decisions is information, we can never have *complete* data. Decisions must be made on the basis of adequate, rather than complete information. The factors that affect how much data can be gathered are, of course, time, energy, and money, all of which are limited resources. One of the skills of a good manager is to be able to judge when there is enough information to make a reasonable decision. There is a clear risk in making a decision on the basis of inadequate data, and there is a less obvious, but nonetheless real, cost of delaying a decision in order to collect additional information. One of the strong arguments for identifying different types of decisions made in a job and putting priorities on them is that this procedure helps to clarify the necessary information base for each decision. If you know, for instance, that you must make certain decisions regarding expenditures, then you can plan to have the data necessary for these decisions available in some easily accessible form. The advent of computerized data-base filing systems has brought the problems of data organization, collection and retrieval into sharp focus—the necessary information is usually there somewhere, but it is very often hard to access unless there has been some very careful prior planning. First, look at the types of decisions that you have to make, and then try to make sure you can obtain the information you or others need to make these decisions.

Personal Values

Needless to say, a significant amount of decision-making is based on emotion rather than on rational thinking. Rational, economic man does not exist; it's a concept used by theorists to discuss decision-making. We are all captives, to some degree, of our values, attitudes, needs, and emotions, and it is difficult to separate these from the way we see things and act on them. M.ach One is designed to help managers look at themselves objectively in order to get a better idea of what motivates them, how they tend to see things, and how they react to certain situations. There is a direct relationship between these factors and the way in which an individual makes decisions. Sometimes that's a good thing, and sometimes it is not. At times we make decisions in a certain way because that's the way we *like* to make them, not because it is the way we *should* make them. Our decision-making "style" is often a reflection of our leadership style, our motivational set, and our values and attitudes.

Like leadership, decision-making processes should be based on the requirements of the particular situation rather than on a preferred method. Different situations require different approaches. Sometimes we have to swallow our personal preferences and do the job the way it should be done rather than the way we'd like to do it, or feel most comfortable doing it. Some decisions *have* to be made by a consensus process if they are to be made properly. Others have to be made by the manager alone, and he or she has to "bite the bullet" and be prepared to live with the consequences. Although personal values can never be set aside completely, the high-achieving manager must attempt to take a more analytic approach to decision-making and must let the *situation* be the major determinant of how a decision is best made. The situation doesn't determine the solution itself, but it does affect the process of decision-making.

Individual vs. Group Decision-Making

The Hollywood-style successful executive is one who sits behind a huge desk making rapid-fire decisions on matters of immense importance. There is never an instant of wavering; his mind works like a computer, spitting out immediate answers to the most complex of problems. He is a truly heroic character and we know that he will carry his ventures through to dazzling success. It's easy to identify the poor managers in these scenarios as well. They're the ones who have difficulty making up their minds, who have doubts about the outcomes of their actions, who go around asking for advice, and who generally take more than two minutes to decide on any issue, no matter how great its magnitude.

Decision-making in the real world, as we all know, isn't like that. The individual who makes a habit of snap decisions is going to get burned, badly and often. The more important the decision, the more time must be allocated to considering the alternatives and all their consequences, and the more time must be given to data collection and analysis. But data collection and consideration of various alternatives are often most effectively carried out by a group of managers who can all focus on the problem at hand, view it from various perspectives, discuss all its possible ramifications, and generate a range of solutions. As described earlier, this was the procedure used by Alfred Sloan when General Motors was faced with its catastrophic drop in sales during the Depression. It was by no means the only way he could have handled the problem—he could have ordered cost cuts, he could have stopped producing certain models, he could have fired a host of people. The difficulty was that GM had never faced such a situation before; it was new and unique and therefore Sloan did not handle it the way he might have handled a more common and routine problem. *When problems are highly complex, when their solution is unclear, when their effects are widespread through the organization, when they are relatively unique or new, and when their resolution requires the action and commitment of a number of other people, they are best made in a group setting.*

Group decision-making is certainly not the only way to go, nor is it always the best way to go. It depends on the circumstances. There are times when decisions are best made by a group, just as there are times when they are best made by a single manager. This is the issue we will discuss next.

Quality of the Decision

A major factor affecting how a decision should be made is the degree to which "quality" of the decision is important. That is, how important is it that this be the *right*, or best decision? In some cases there are a number of relatively similar alternatives; it doesn't matter much which one is chosen. For instance, how important is it to choose one particular present over another for an employee who has just had a baby? There are a number of suitable gifts, any one of which would be appropriate. Quality refers to the "correctness" of the decision in purely objective and impersonal terms. Is it the right decision, other factors notwithstanding?

In some cases, the quality of a decision is critical. It *must* be right, because the consequences of making the wrong decision are too great to risk. For instance, two decisions that had quite different results, but that were equally critical to the organizations involved, were Ford's decision to produce the Edsel and Xerox's decision to produce the 9000 series of copiers. Both decisions involved immense amounts of money. The first one proved to be ill-advised and cost the Ford Motor Company dearly, while the second proved to be right and made a major contribution to the revenues and profits of the Xerox Corporation. When hundreds of millions of dollars are at stake, the importance of making a *quality* decision is paramount.

On a more general level, decisions to buy certain machinery, to launch various promotional or marketing plans, or to hire or fire certain types of people can also be critical. The "right" decision in each of these instances is important. We're all familiar with evaluating decisions. Because no one wants to make the *wrong* decision, quality is often uppermost in our minds. We believe that once the "right" decision is made, everything will fall in place. The critical point appears to be making the decision, for it is assumed that everything else will flow naturally. Unfortunately, this just isn't true. As every manager knows (and we all seem to have learned it the hard way), a decision made is not necessarily a decision implemented. It takes the actions of others to carry out a decision, and this is often much harder to accomplish than it was to make the decision in the first place.

Acceptance of the Decision

A second factor critical to the success of many decisions is the acceptance of the decision. Acceptance means that those affected by a decision are committed to its implementation. Is this decision attractive and reasonable to the people who must work with it? Are they willing to live with it? A decision may be "correct" in the eyes of the manager who makes it, and in the eyes of top management, but if the people who have to implement it resist it, tremendous problems can occur. An individual can only do so much and can only influence others to a certain extent. If people don't want to accept a decision, its intended objectives become difficult to achieve.

Unfortunately, many managers see no correlation between the quality of a decision and its degree of acceptance. A good decision, they argue, may not necessarily be a popular one, but it is the duty of subordinates to carry it out. We know, however, that emotions also influence decisions, so why wouldn't the people who are affected by these decisions also be swayed by emotion? Subordinates have feelings just as their bosses do, so that their reactions to certain decisions may at times seem "irrational." Managers may not understand why some directions aren't carried out. It's not that they haven't been understood, and it's not that they *can't* be carried out; it's just that for some reason subordinates don't *want* to carry out the directions.

Managers aren't paid to make decisions. They are paid to *have decisions implemented*. If commitment is critical, then a manager should make his or her decision in a way that ensures commitment. The relative importance of quality and acceptance determine to a large extent the way in which decisions should be made. Decision-making, like the other aspects of management that we have talked about, depends on the situation. There are ways of making decisions in certain situations that work better than others.

Time Constraints

Time is often an overriding factor in managerial situations. Everything has to be done yesterday. It may be difficult to distinguish a real emergency from a so-called emergency because everyone thinks that what he or she has to do should be first in line. We all have a fear of waiting endlessly to accomplish the most trivial things. But because the major cause of rushed decisions is lack of planning, we can be held accountable for many of our own "panics."

There are a number of useful time-management techniques to help us eliminate such panics. First, one needs to know where time is spent on the job. Keeping a time log for a few weeks can be an extremely revealing exercise, for it will show the various ways in which we fritter away time. The ten and fifteen minutes here and there that are spent finding things, changing from one activity to another, carrying on conversations for too long, going to and from meetings, and so on, add up to a considerable portion of the day. We sometimes blame our colleagues for interruptions but forget that if we closed the door, or had all calls directed through a secretary, many of these interruptions would never have the chance to occur. Time is wasted in different ways by different people. Find out how you allocate your time. And remember the 20/80 rule as you do so.

Even the way you make decisions can be a major time waster. Some managers spend endless hours in meetings to decide matters that could have been decided individually in minutes. They fear that they will be tarred with the brush of autocracy, and they want to make sure that everyone in their unit feels he or she is able to participate to the fullest extent in all decisions. The only problem is that not everyone wants to participate in every decision. Most of us would like to be a part of certain decisions, but are quite happy to let others be made by someone else. Some managers, reacting strongly to what they perceive as a huge time waster, make all decisions themselves. Unfortunately, this approach often wastes just as much time because of the interminable haggles, arguments, resistances, and fights over implementing such unilateral decisions.

Make no mistake—time can be a critical dimension in making a decision. Deadlines are deadlines, and there are occasions when the situation is sprung on you without much warning, and you have to come up with an answer right away. There are many instances of genuine time pressure. But beware also of false time pressures—pressures generated either by others who wish to make you react faster than you want to or should, or pressures generated by yourself simply because you are impatient or want to make decisions on your own and so let time shortage become a convenient excuse. When time is genuinely short, you have to act. When you have some leeway—and it doesn't have to be very great—you can involve others in the decision-making process, where appropriate.

EFFECTIVE DECISION-MAKING

Among the numerous factors that affect decision-making, two of the basic underlying dimensions are the *quality* of the decision and its *acceptance*. If we focus on these two issues, bearing in mind the need for an adequate information base and the effects of our own personal values (and those of others), we can develop a simple but comprehensive approach to making decisions.

Traditionally, we have been led to believe that the effectiveness of decisions rests primarily on *quality*. We are supposed to (1) identify the problem, (2) gather information, (3) weigh and consider various alternative solutions, and (4) make a decision. This process implies that there is a correct decision, and that once it is made everyone will accept it as appropriate and act accordingly. In technological situations these assumptions are often true, but where people are involved in the implementation of the decision, quality is no longer the only issue: *acceptance* becomes a very important factor.

Effective decisions are those that (a) identify the best solution to a problem in quantitative, factual terms, and (b) have the most desirable outcomes, given the circumstances. Often these two conditions are in opposition to one another. What is "best" for the manager or the organization may not be seen as "best" for the individuals and groups involved. We sometimes know what would be ideal, but we also know that the ideal can't be achieved. What we have to strive for is the best possible outcome *in the circumstances*, and often the circumstances have to do with what people will commit themselves to.

In today's environment, there is more and more pressure toward making acceptance an initial target to strive for. To achieve acceptance, however, it becomes necessary to share decision-making with subordinates, and many managers perceive this as a risky strategy. They are afraid of losing control of the decision, since they are held ultimately responsible for results, so they wish to retain some veto power. Although this approach may be appropriate in many circumstances, subordinates often suspect that their managers are merely pretending to discuss an issue with them, that their participation is sought only as long as the outcome is in agreement with what the bosses wanted to happen anyway. How can we resolve the question of when to make a decision by consensus, by consultation, or by direct command?

TYPES OF PROBLEMS AND STYLES OF DECISION-MAKING

Problems can be examined with respect to the degree to which quality and acceptance are important. Although individuals may disagree on the relative importance of these two factors, the manager making the decision is the one who is ultimately responsible and who must evaluate the situation. If, for instance, you think that a certain decision *must* be made and there are no other suitable alternatives, then you should not invite participation; simply make the decision and be done with it. We call this the *command* decision-making style and it is perfectly legitimate and often the best strategy. Pretending to listen to the opinions of others—false participation—is a high-risk strategy, because, as we all know, you can only fool some of the people some of the time, and when they find out, they become very annoyed. If, on the other hand, you favor a certain decision but are still open to argument, your actions should be different. Ask for people's opinions, but make it clear that you reserve the right to make the final decision. This is the *consultation* style of decision-making. Finally, when you have some opinions but think that other valid viewpoints are available, that a final decision should take into account the ideas and informed opinions of other people, and that the people involved would appreciate having a say in the final outcome, the *consensus* approach is most appropriate.

What we've been saying, of course, is that the way you make a decision—by command, consultation, or consensus—depends on the situation. In this case, we are using only two main factors to define the situation: quality and acceptance. Those are the two that every manager must be concerned with. Is the decision the right one, and will people go along with it? On the basis of the relative importance of these two factors, we can suggest an "ideal" style of decision-making:

1. If quality of the decision is more important than its acceptance, then a *command* style is most appropriate.

2. If quality and acceptance are *both* important, then a *consultation* style is most appropriate.

3. If acceptance is more important than quality, then a *consensus* style is most appropriate.

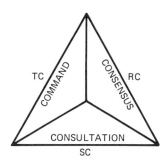

Figure 5-2. The Decision Style Triangle

As illustrated in Figure 5-2, each of these "styles" of decision-making is related to an underlying style of management. The command style is essentially task-centered, the consultation style is essentially situation-centered, and the consensus style is basically relationship-centered.

Once again, we can establish a link between leadership behavior, motivation, decision-making style, *and the job.* Jobs that require a basic task-centered approach, where *control, direction, production, performance, persuasion,* and *implementation* are important, are jobs in which the leadership style of the *benevolent autocrat* is appropriate, where motivation is derived to a large extent from a *need for achievement,* and where the individual in charge must make decisions by using a *command* style.

When the job requires a basic situation-centered approach, and *coordination, planning, negotiation, strategy,* and *change* are important elements, motivation is derived largely from a *need for power,* the appropriate leadership style is that of the *professional,* and decisions are best made using a *consultation* style.

By the same token, when the job involves a great deal of *advice, collaboration, discussion, encouragement, guidance, innovation*, and the like, motivation is centered on a *need for affiliation*, managerial behavior is oriented toward an *instructor* style, and decisions are best made using a *consensus* approach.

There is a necessary and basic consistency to good management. Depending on the situation, the way a manager leads, motivates, communicates, and makes decisions must form a certain pattern; inconsistency and unpredictability are unsettling and lead to low levels of achievement.

TIME AND TRUST AS MITIGATING FACTORS

We have already talked about time as a dominant influence on managerial behavior. It is the one limited, nonrenewable resource we all have to deal with. We have to budget and use it carefully, for it often changes the nature of managerial situations. For instance, when time is highly critical, when there is a terrific rush to complete a project, the relative roles of quality and acceptance become less important. If there is little time available, you have to use a command style; you simply cannot afford to have group meetings or consult a number of other people. But beware of how you assess the criticality of the time dimension. We all tend to be in too much of a rush, and we have all learned to expect everything yesterday, even if it's not important. Many managers use time as an *excuse* for making command decisions when they could be consulting others and obtaining some consensus on a proposed action. When time becomes absolutely critical, even if acceptance is important, the individual manager has to make the decisions using a command style. Just make sure, however, that you don't abuse the time factor and give it more weight than it really requires.

The second mitigating factor in decision-making is *trust*. Whenever there is a high level of trust between you and your subordinates, you can use any of the three basic decision-making styles. That is to say, you will not be perceived to be acting against the wishes of the group, or to be doing things inappropriately. This means that in certain circumstances you may forego the need for consensus on a specific decision and simply make the decision yourself. You may know what the overall view is anyway, and you may know the best course of action. If your subordinates trust you, they will accept your decision and will not be bothered by not having a chance to participate. On the other hand, if you call your subordinates together to make a consensus decision on a matter that really doesn't require a high degree of acceptance, they will trust you enough to know you are doing this for a good reason. You may wish to have the group meet merely to foster a feeling of camaraderie among them, or to reassure them of your respect for them.

But, like time, the element of trust can be abused. Don't assume your subordinates are so trusting that you can blithely make command decisions or drag them to meeting after meeting for no particular reason other than the fact you have a scheduled slot for it. As a good manager you should build a bank of trust with your subordinates, but just make sure you make more deposits than withdrawals.

The benefit of deep trust between managers and subordinates is that it gives the manager considerable flexibility in the way he or she operates. This is tremendously important. There are times when a manager needs to react rapidly and differently to situations. If you're unable to get subordinates to accept quick changes, as is often the case where highly organized unions and tight regulations exist, decision-making is considerably more difficult. If your subordinates trust you they will accept a certain degree of variability in the decisions you make, and you can achieve much more.

This is one of the "secrets" that Japanese management has discovered. Managers and subordinates in Japan work closely together under a strong bond of trust. As a result, if a rapid decision has to be made, there is a degree of acceptance and understanding that we in the West find amazing. The Japanese strive for consensus most of the time. They're willing to pay the front-end cost of the time involved in order to ensure acceptance of major decisions. But it would be a mistake to think that *all* their decisions are made in this way. They have to react quickly at times, just as managers in the West do. The advantage that they have in these situations, though, is that they have already spent some time building up high levels of trust within their groups and organizations, so that when they have to make a fast command decision, it's acceptable. They don't have the problems that arise in some of our companies when a management decision taken on the spot, for example, leads to a sudden walkout by workers. High trust gives a manager tremendous flexibility in decision-making; low trust gives none.

DECISION-MAKING AND THE M.ACH ONE SYSTEM

Figure 5-3 shows how the relative importance of Quality, Acceptance, Time, and Trust determines decision-making style within the M.ach One system. As you proceed through the model you must decide whether each of these factors is of *major* or *minor* importance in the situation under consideration. These decisions will lead you through the branches of the model to the appropriate decision style.

An important point to remember about decision-making, from the point of view of M.ach One, is that it is directly related to the situation, to your managerial style, and to your motivational set. As we know, individuals with a high need for achievement like to get on with things by themselves. Therefore it is not unusual to see them use the command style of decision-making more often than necessary. Their task-centered style of management spills over into the way they make decisions. They tend to have a lower concern for relationships and people, and they don't see the need for consultation or consensus. The same is true, of course, for individuals who are strongly relationship- or situation-centered. Their style of decision-making matches their underlying motivational set and behavior patterns.

Motivational drives are difficult to alter. Style of behavior is hard to change, but is easier to alter than motivation. Decision-making style is the easiest of the three to adjust to the demands of the situation. If decisions are the most visible part of your job, then a rapid way to increase achievement is to make better decisions. Sort them out in terms of priority, who should make them, and how they should be made, and you'll be well on the way to operating at a higher level of effectiveness. Exercise 5-2 contains the scoring key for the Decision Style Inventory. Score yourself and see how well you are able to assess situations and make the appropriate style of decisions. You may find it useful to go over the various situations and reassess them in the light of what you now know about the concepts of quality, acceptance, time, and trust. You may find that you would respond differently.

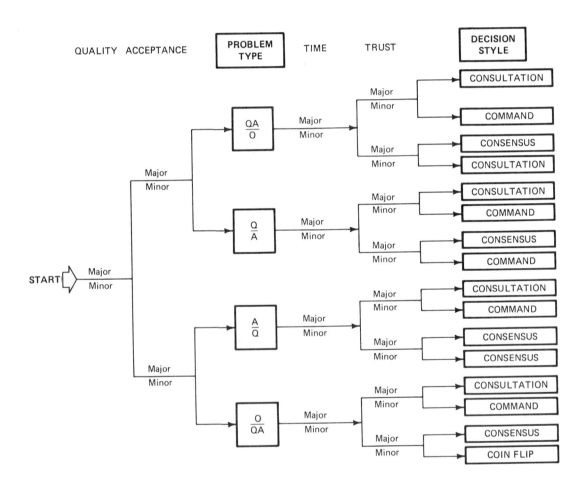

Figure 5-3. The M.ach One Decision-Making Model

Exercise 5-2.   Analyze your Decision Style Inventory

Quality and Acceptance

As you know, how you make a decision depends on a variety of factors. Two of the more important ones are the degree to which *quality* of the decision (it's "rightness"), and *acceptance* (its attractiveness to those affected) are important. The relative weighting of these two factors is a basic determinant of decision-making style, as indicated in Figure 5-3.

When Quality of the decision is much more important than gaining acceptance for it (Q/A), a Command style is most appropriate. Make sure you make the right decision, and get on with it.

When Acceptance is the major issue, and the actual "correctness" of the decision is less important (A/Q), a Consensus style is best because it gets everyone involved and committed.

When both Quality and Acceptance are important (QA/O), a Consultation style is most appropriate because it incorporates elements of involvement and commitment from those affected, and at the same time you can exert some control over the decision by reserving the right to make it yourself.

There is also the case where *neither* of these two factors are important (O/QA). A situation where this is the case is the following:

> It has been decided that employees should be encouraged to participate in some kind of physical fitness program. This will be purely on a voluntary basis, but any employee who is interested will have his or her membership paid in a health club. There are two clubs close to the organization's offices, and large group rates can be negotiated with both. There is very little difference between the rates, and the facilities are quite similar in each. Because of the numbers needed to get a favorable group rate, membership can only be offered in one of the two clubs. You are to decide which health club the organization will buy membership in.

Clearly, the Quality of the decision is not much of an issue here: both clubs offer similar advantages. And Acceptance is not particularly important because membership is voluntary, so that those who want it can have it, and those that don't are not inconvenienced. In this case any decision-making style will suffice. In actuality, you would probably delegate this to someone else while you got on with more pressing matters.

Time and Trust

The two other mitigating factors in decision-making are Time and Trust. These have been commented on in the body of the chapter, but essentially, the effect they have on the decision-making process is that:

- When Time is critical, Command decisions become more necessary. You simply cannot afford the luxury of getting a variety of opinions, or going through a lengthy consensus process.

- When Trust in the manager is very high, you can vary your style to suit your needs, using Command decisions and still getting high degrees of acceptance, etc.

Analysis of the 5 Situations

When you responded to the situations in Exercise 5-1, we had not discussed the issues of Quality, Acceptance, Time, and Trust. You probably decided how to act on an intuitive basis, or on the basis of your experience to date. Therefore your rationale for making the decisions as you did is likely very different from what is presented below. However, take a look at what you suggested doing and what we suggest, and compare the two. You should get a feel for the relative importance of the factors we have included in the M.ach One model.

Situation 1: A Command Decision. The *quality* of your decision in this case is absolutely critical! You must price this product correctly. There is no indication that acceptance of the pricing decision by other areas in the organization is likely to be a special problem. You have the necessary data and therefore this is clearly a decision you must take yourself.

Situation 2: A Command Decision. Because this process was developed by your people as a team, there is some indication that their involvement in the decision as to its present marketability would be desirable, purely from a morale maintenance standpoint. These are creative, energetic young people, and they are motivated to an extent by the importance superiors attach to them. Certainly, being consulted on the marketability of "their" product is something they would expect and enjoy. However, in this case you are constrained by the *time* element. It is already late in the day, and many of the group may have left. If this is the case, you have to make the decision yourself and ride with it. Of course, if you can reach a few by phone for a quick conversation, by all means do so, but the decision rests with you.

Situation 3: A Consensus Decision. There is some question whether the proposed group-based incentive system will be any better than the old one in terms of productivity, and therefore *quality* of the decision is not clearly an important factor. On the other hand, from the point of view of the loggers, this plan represents a significant change, and if they resist it strongly, productivity could suffer. It would appear that getting their *acceptance* to the plan is of paramount importance. Once that's done, business can continue as usual and any bugs can be ironed out as things progress.

Situation 4: A Consultation Decision. Here is an instance where you have to be careful to make the "right" decision, and at the same time, you have to be careful that you don't lose your entire salesforce and your shipper by overreacting. You would like the practice to cease, but it is not specifically against company rules. You will have to tread carefully here. Discussion and consultation would appear to be key elements in the decision-making process in this situation.

Situation 5: A Consultation Decision. You have some leeway here because of the high bond of loyalty and trust exhibited by the employees. They know you well, have worked for the company for a long time, and know that they will not be taken advantage of. Make the decision the way you prefer, but be sure not to make this the first time the employees end up on the short end. If the decision is essentially equitable and is good for the company, there will not be any great amount of resistance to it. People can accept decisions that don't favor them personally if they trust the people making these decisions and recognize that the criteria are basically fair.

6

The Manager
Is the Message

The majority of problems in organizations have some basis in poor communication. Almost without fail, when managers are asked to diagnose what went wrong in a situation, one of the items they list is a "communication breakdown." Unfortunately, although managers may recognize that the appropriate message has not been sent or received, they usually don't know what to do about it other than to meet with the people involved and discuss the problem. The truth is that almost every management problem is a "communication" problem, but the term itself is so vague that it's usually not very helpful in attempting to deal with the situation. However, we must come to grips with the issue of communication because it is the basis for all management action—you simply cannot manage others without communicating with them.

There is far more to communication than simply supplying information. British Intelligence reputedly knew of the Argentinian invasion of the Falkland Islands weeks in advance, but the government failed to act on the information. Similarly, the CIA had all the information necessary to assess the situation before the Cuban missile crisis in 1962, but failed to process it adequately in time to avoid the ultimate confrontation. The history of communications problems is endless. The fate of nations has turned on single instances of communications either received and acted on appropriately, or missed and misinterpreted.

How do you communicate with the people around you? Do they always know what you want them to do, how you feel about things, which jobs are urgent and which are routine, when you would like special care taken with a task, what emphasis you would like placed on certain activities, or what approach you think is most appropriate in tackling certain problems? Are your communications as clear to the *recipients* as they are to you? Are your memos always understood? Do they convey meanings that you did not intend? Take the following memo, for instance:

TO: All Department Managers
FROM: Doug Simms, V-P Finance
SUBJECT: Cost Reduction

The comptroller's committee has reviewed our profitability over the past year. As you know, economic conditions for the coming year are at best unpredictable. This uncertainty we feel will put pressure on our profitability.

We recognize the problems inherent in attempting to reduce expenses; however we are asking you to continue to press to reduce expenditures, particularly those that are not specifically assignable to particular contracts. While I am reluctant to establish specific goals, I would suggest a reduction of 8 percent to 12 percent.

I would like to emphasize that we do not wish to interfere with essential activities or to participate directly in determining what specific kinds of expenses should be attacked.

That looks like a pretty clear memo, doesn't it? The vice-president of finance wants an average cost reduction of 10 percent in general administrative overheads. Or is that the way you interpreted it? He is concerned about finances and has already budgeted the 10 percent administrative cost reduction into the figures for the coming year, and this has been approved by the budget committee and is now being made part of the profit targets for the year. Or didn't you understand that to be the case? People who do not attack cost reductions right away, and who fail to achieve a minimum level of 8 percent savings can expect trouble. That was unstated but clear, wasn't it? So really there was no difficulty with this memo. You, as a manager in this organization, understand exactly what is wanted and precisely what is going to happen, don't you? The vice-president's expectations are clear, and he is going to get just what he wants. Right?

As you might suspect, some people understood this memo to mean one thing and others took a completely different view of it. When the cost reductions began, some were adequate and some weren't. Some were directed toward the right areas and others weren't. Some people failed to understand that there was very little leeway as to the amount they could or should cut, and there was a great deal of acrimony when the boom was lowered by the budget committee later in the year. The *intention* was good, but the communication was inadequate.

COMMUNICATION AS THE MEDIUM FOR MANAGEMENT

The way you communicate is part of your style of management. In fact, you cannot lead, motivate, or make and implement decisions without communicating. Communication is the medium managers use to do their jobs. Your words, your memos, your actions, gestures, and expressions—all serve as messages to the people around you. They interpret these messages and act accordingly. The process is complex, and the whole range and variety of messages you transmit is taken into account, weighed, compared, and evaluated. *The manager is the message*—the whole package of spoken and written words, nonverbal actions, attitudes, gestures, presentation, and expression.

We use communication for two basic purposes:

1. To influence and change the behavior, values, and attitudes, of others.

2. To maintain and protect our own behavior, values, and attitudes.

We *transmit* as well as *receive* communications, and in each instance, they are *filtered* and *modified* to fit the situation and the needs of the people or groups involved. We know that people tend to hear what they want to hear, and not what they don't want to hear. In the memo from the vice-president of finance, the individuals who wanted to crack down hard on costs tended to "hear" that in the message, while others who felt they had already cut back as much as they could in their departments chose to "hear" a request, but not a command, and they were very distressed when they were reprimanded for not cutting back enough. They hadn't thought the cuts were critical, and hoped that their particular departments might be spared. We've all seen reactions of this type. People interpret the same communication differently. What we need to know is why this happens.

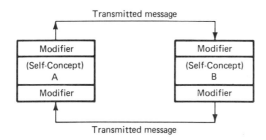

Figure 6-1. A Simplified Model of the Communication Process

Figure 6-1 shows a simplified model of the communication process and illustrates the way we tend to modify messages, either as we send them or receive them. Imagine yourself as manager A. The way in which you transmit messages depends on your values, attitudes, your overall style, and even your mood at the moment. Therefore if you wish to convey a message such as the one in the memo we just looked at, you can choose *how* you're going to get your point across. The basic message you want to convey in this example is that all department managers are to cut general administrative costs by an average of 10 percent. You have to decide whether to explain why, whether to clarify what you mean by "general administrative costs," whether to put special emphasis on the importance of the cost cuts, whether to outline the penalties for not achieving the cuts, whether to state the rewards for implementing the decision, whether to invite responses from the recipients of the memo, and so on. You *modify* the message in many ways to reflect your attitude and objectives, and you do so in your own style.

If you usually consult your people and solicit their opinions and suggestions, you might do so here as well by calling a meeting or inviting written suggestions as to how the cuts can be made. If you think this decision has to be made and acted upon immediately, you may word it in a more task-centered way so as to reflect the sense of urgency you feel. What you are doing in each of these cases is *modifying the way in which you transmit the*

message, so that it influences other people to change their behavior and at-
titudes.

Now put yourself in the position of manager B, the recipient of the
message. As manager B, you will interpret this memo in terms of your own
values, attitudes, needs, and style. If, for instance, you are new in your job
as a department manager and uncertain about your future, you will likely
perceive a threat in the memo. He *says* he doesn't want to dictate where
costs are to be reduced, but you may not be so sure about that. And he
"suggests" a reduction of 8-12 percent, but does that mean something
stronger? If you're new and unsure about how things operate in your job,
you're not likely to take too many chances. You will interpret the message
by "hearing" certain things, and screening out others, so that it fits your
perception of yourself and your job.

To illustrate this process, imagine the same memo being read by an old
hand who has been around for years, is widely experienced in the company,
and feels secure and powerful in his or her job. This manager will interpret
the message quite differently. Perhaps it will be seen as simply another of
those annual appeals for budget cuts—if you ignore them, they forget about
you and go away. The veteran manager's responses are likely to be different
from the new manager's. *We screen the communications we receive and we*
use the communications we transmit to maintain and protect our own
values, attitudes, needs, and goals.

COMMUNICATION IN ORGANIZATIONS

Life in an organization is structured by the roles assigned to individuals, by
the hierarchical relationships between members, and by authority and status
differences. This structure in turn affects communications and problem
solving. Research shows that centralized organizations and groups solve
relatively simple problems quicker and more accurately than decentralized
organizations. The latter, however, handle complex problems better, faster,
and with a higher degree of satisfaction for the people involved. All that this
means, of course, is that when people pool their efforts in the solution of
complex problems, everyone has a contribution to make, has some "ownership" of the solution, and feels committed to doing a good job. We know,
however, that a decentralized, group approach to problem solving is not
always appropriate, and therefore we need to take the research data on
communications with some degree of reservation. If the problem is so complex that a variety of expertise and a good deal of acceptance are needed in
order to progress, then the research findings make sense. We should involve
people, listen as well as talk to them and use either a strong consultation
style or strive for consensus.

Communication, in a managerial sense, involves some action whereby
the sender of a message obtains an effect on the part of the receiver. We are
concerned with the *behavior* that results from a communication—how it influences the people around us to act in one way or another. Therefore, in

discussing communication we must first look at its underlying goals, and then consider how to achieve these goals.

FUNCTIONS OF COMMUNICATION

Communication serves different functions and has several underlying goals. Of course, all communication is concerned with influencing the behavior and attitudes of others or with maintaining our own behavior and attitudes. The basic aim of communication is merely to *provide information*. We simply want to let people know certain things that we think they need to know in order to do their jobs. (But remember that even at this basic level the process may involve attempts to influence the behavior of others. *We* decide what information is "needed" so that people will be more likely to do what we want them to do.) At another level, the goal of communication may be to *influence and persuade* others—rather than to transmit pure information, the message is intended to "sell" an idea or course of action. And finally, we use communication to *order and direct* the behavior of others. Instead of persuading them to do what we want done we are simply "telling" them what to do.

But all these functions of communication are determined by the viewpoint of the initiator of the message. We talk about providing information, influencing and persuading, or ordering and directing, but what about *receiving* information, or *being influenced*? We have to obtain feedback from somewhere, and there has to be an upward flow of information in the organization to let us know what is going on, what results are being achieved, and what problems are being encountered. At some point we have to *listen* —that is, we have to be on the receiving end of the communication.

COMMUNICATION STYLE

A manager's style of communication reveals a great deal about that individual. Some managers communicate mainly downward, initiating most conversations, putting forward most suggestions, ideas, and orders, telling subordinates what to do, and how and when to do it. Others do more listening, let subordinates initiate communication, and encourage and support their ideas and suggestions. And a third group initiate and receive communications about equally; they listen as much as they talk, discuss ideas and suggestions, and integrate and coordinate the information and proposals put forward within their group. It's not a question of which of these styles is "best." Like leadership, motivation, or decision-making, the most effective style of communication is the one that suits the requirements of the situation.

One of the major determining factors affecting communication is its *direction*. Within an organization we can talk about communication being either *downward, upward, or horizontal*. We are probably most familiar with downward communication because from an early age we have been told things by people who are bigger, more senior, or more powerful than us. Organizations are structured in such a way that a great deal of the communication is downward. Managers tell subordinates what their jobs are, appraise their performance, dispense rewards and punishments, and act as sources of information, power, and authority. Downward communication is concerned with telling subordinates who is to do what, how, and when. It is task-centered. The superior does most of the talking, writing, and acting, and the subordinates do most of the listening, reading, and observing. Goals, plans, and objectives flow down from the top, and employees are told where they fit in the organization and what they have to do. The communication style is *telling*, the underlying objective is *direction*, and the behavior is essentially *task-centered*.

Horizontal communication, as the term implies, takes place between peers, or members of a team, across functions and departments, and it is less constrained by status, level, and authority differences. It is often less formal in content. Studies indicate that managers spend considerable time communicating in this fashion with friends and colleagues throughout the organization, asking for and giving favors, making informal deals, and bypassing the often cumbersome formal chain of command. This type of communication is based on *discussion*, its underlying objectives are *integration and coordination*, and the behavior is basically *situation-centered*.

Most managers pay lip service to the concept of *upward* communication and maintain that "my office door is always open" and "I need feedback on how things are going." But when it comes right down to it, few managers actually foster and encourage such communication. They find it easier to tell others what to do, to give them feedback, and to appraise their performance, than to be on the receiving end. Remember, we attempt to influence others and protect ourselves. However, feedback is essential, and we need to have an accurate picture of what is really going on in our divisions, departments, or groups. Being cut off from this type of information exacts a terrible price. Richard Nixon's major mistake was his failure to find out what was going on outside his office. The information that reached him was so distorted that he based his decisions on incorrect data, which no doubt caused him to take the seemingly irrational steps that led to his demise as president. More than one corporate executive has fallen victim to the same mistake. Somehow, upward communication must be obtained.

Upward communication doesn't mean that you, the manager, transmit messages up the hierarchy. It means that your job is to make sure that subordinates transmit messages upward to you. As a manager, you initiate a lot of communication; you talk, write, and act a great deal. Your role in these transactions tends to be one of a transmitter rather than receiver. But if you believe that your subordinates have important messages, that they should come to you for help with problems, that they should be interested in generating ideas for improving productivity and systems, and that they should let you know when things are going badly as well as when they're going well, then you have to adopt a style that fosters upward communication. This style is characterized by *listening* rather than talking, and its underlying objective is to *encourage and support* the behavior of subordinates rather than to direct or coordinate it. This style is essentially a *relationship-centered* approach.

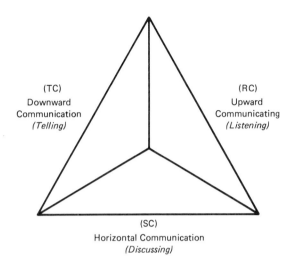

Figure 6-2. Communication Style Related to the M.ach One Model

Communication style can be related to the basic M.ach One model (Figure 6-2). Just as leadership, motivation, and decision-making can be related to the three underlying dimensions of managerial behavior, so, obviously, can communication. Communication *is* leadership, motivation, and decision-making. It is *how* managers do all those things. It is the medium for influencing behavior, and therefore it is an integral *part of* leadership, motivation, and decision-making. To separate communication from these concepts makes little sense. We communicate in order to make things happen, and we call this process leadership, motivation, or decision-making, depending on the form the communication takes and the basic objectives it attempts to achieve.

What M.ach One does, above all else, is point out clearly that management is not a disjointed process. Managerial achievement is *not* the product of a set of "cookbook" techniques. It is the integration of a complete and wholistic approach to the management of people. Its basis is the job—the situation the manager is faced with. Careful attention to the behavioral requirements of the job, and a clear and, above all, *consistent* approach to managing the people concerned—motivating them, leading them, communicating with them, and making the decisions that will guide their actions—is what leads to high managerial achievement. It is a matter of doing the right things with the right people, in the right way, at the right time. It can be done—and you can do it.

7

Compatibility and Achievement: Matching Yourself to the Job

Throughout this book we've made the point that high achievement is the result of handling critical requirements of the job appropriately. But just what do we mean by that statement? How exactly must overall style match the job? At what level of detail are we working? Certainly, the closer the fit, the higher the potential level of achievement; if you understand the precise requirements for getting the job done well and you meet those requirements exactly, you must, by definition, achieve excellent results. Compatibility is a key element in managerial achievement. Not compatibility in the usual sense of the word, which is compatibility with people, but in the sense of matching your behavior to the demands of your job.

Some examples may serve to illustrate what we mean. The manager of a government agency might have a job that is primarily concerned with establishing a clear *strategy* for the agency, *forecasting* needs and costs, *planning* and *coordinating* programs, *negotiating* packages, and *evaluating* performance. All of these elements might be considered *essential* to the success of the agency. In addition, the manager might think that he or she has to provide *guidance, encouragement,* and *advice* to employees in order to keep them working well, but that these aspects of the job have lower priority. The predominant requirements of this job are situation-centered (the top priority elements are all SC—see the critical achievement elements in Table 1-1). But there is also a need for a small amount of relationship-centeredness, since the lower priority elements are all RC.

If, in the above case, the manager's style happens to be largely that of the Benevolent Autocrat (TC +), there would be little compatibility between the demands of the job and the manager's style. Being a Benevolent Autocrat means the manager would tend to be a dominant figure, would like to give direction, and would be determined, energetic, and compelling. Communication would be largely downward, and most decisions would be made in a Command style. The picture emerges of an individual who is an overpowering "salesman," trying to get everyone to do things the way he or she thinks is best, while the job actually requires a far more detached perspective. What this manager really needs to do is stand back from the day-to-day operating details and look at the overall questions of strategy and policy. This job requires the sort of activity that takes place in the operations room during wartime—it requires assessing the total picture and planning a comprehensive response to it, rather than getting down on the firing line and becoming enveloped in the events of the moment.

Let's assume that the manager is also mildly relationship-centered and exhibits the style of diplomat (RC 0) to a slight degree. Given that RC

112
Compatibility
and
Achievement:
Matching
Yourself
to the Job

behavior is important but not critical to the job, the manager might be able to at least handle the interpersonal aspect of his work reasonably well. People's annoyance at this manager's dominance and interference on the job might be lessened by his seeming concern for relationships. But in the final analysis, the agency's objectives would not be met, simply because of inadequate attention to strategy, planning, and other important matters. No amount of interpersonal skill would be able to overcome that failing.

This is an example of low compatibility between the job and the manager's style. Although behavior matches job demands to *some* extent, the critical areas are not covered. The things that absolutely *must* be done won't be done, and things that are unnecessary and often counterproductive will absorb the energies of both the manager and his or her subordinates. We all know individuals whose styles are incompatible with the jobs they hold. They are too soft when they should be hard, too hard when they should be softer, too analytical when they should be action-oriented, and so on. We readily find such examples among the people around us because they are all low achievers in their jobs. Being low achievers, they are the target of considerable attention and pressure, but they don't seem to change, and we don't know why. The answer may be that their managerial style simply does not match the demands of their jobs.

What about your own job? You've had an opportunity to think about it and to analyze it in terms of its nine critical achievement elements. What sort of approach does it appear to require of you? On the basis of your results on the Management Style Behavior Test, how does your leadership style fit your job? Is your approach to making decisions and to communication congruent with the requirements of the job? Does the job contain the things that you find motivating? Look at the list of critical achievement elements you decided on in Exercise 2-4 and see if you can determine your compatibility with your job.

ASSESSING COMPATIBILITY GRAPHICALLY

We can get a picture of the degree of compatibility between a manager and his or her job by using the M.ach One triangles. The techniques we discussed for plotting both style and job in Chapters 2 and 3 are used. The *job* of the manager of the government agency would like triangle (a) in Figure 7-1. The manager's *style* would look like triangle (b).

These two triangles show that there is very little overlap between the required behavior in the job and the behavior shown by the manager. How can this individual possibly attain a high level of achievement in his or her job? Almost every action the manager takes goes against the grain. The job will almost certainly degenerate into a mad series of "firefights" as the manager jumps from one problem situation to another and attempts to bring short-term solutions to problems and issues that are long-term in nature.

To illustrate the concept of compatibility further, let's look at another example. Figure 7-2 shows a manager whose style and job are also incom-

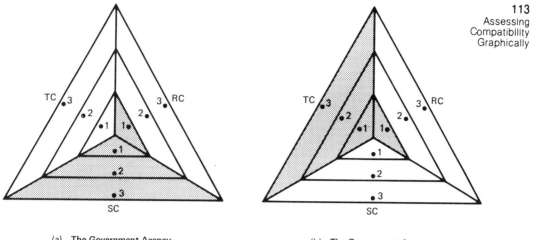

(a) The Government Agency
    Manager's Job

(b) The Government Agency
    Manager's Style

Figure 7-1. An Example of Low Compatibility between Job and Style. This manager will not achieve the major required outputs of the job.

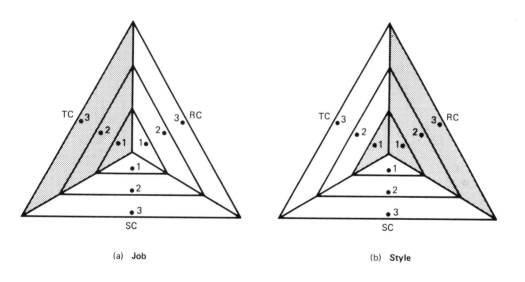

(a) Job

(b) Style

Figure 7-2. An Example of Incompatibility between Job and Style. The manager in this situation is too relationship-centered. The basic style required is task-centered.

114
Compatibility
and
Achievement:
Matching
Yourself
to the Job

patible, but for different reasons. This time the job requires a basic task-centered approach, but the manager is largely relationship-centered, and shows no task-centered behavior at all. This manager has little chance of achieving results in the critical areas of the job. The manager is focusing on things like *advice, consultation, encouragement, morale,* and *training* (all RC elements), but not on the things that are considered essential in the job, such as *control, direction, persuasion, production,* and *performance* (all TC elements).

In this case the manager is too people-oriented when that approach simply isn't required. This manager assumes that subordinates want and need to be involved in the work, should contribute to decisions, have a lot of useful information to communicate, and want to feel part of a group. But, as we know, some jobs just aren't like that, and some people aren't like that. There are times when, as a subordinate, you know that the situation is beyond your grasp, and yet you know that success depends on having everyone in the unit do their specific jobs properly. The only person who can assure successful performance is a superior who has a complete grasp of the situation. Therefore you expect clear and timely directives that you are prepared to carry out without much questioning. Any one who has been in one of the armed services knows that when the action starts, you rely on good officers and NCOs to get you through in one piece. Often the same type of interaction is called for in civilian organizations.

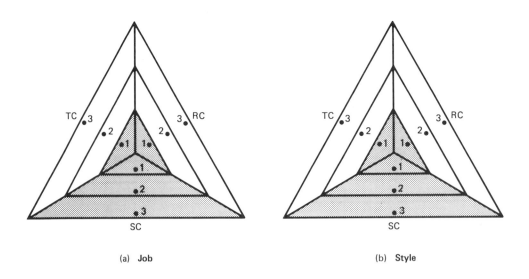

(a) Job   (b) Style

Figure 7-3. An Example of High Compatibility between Job and Style. This manager is likely to be a high achiever in his or her job.

The third example (see Figure 7-3) illustrates a situation in which the manager has a high degree of compatibility with the job. The job requires a great deal of situation-centered behavior (3 degrees of SC), and small amounts of both relationship-centered and task-centered behavior (1 degree of each), and that is *exactly* the type of behavior the manager exhibits. It is a perfect match.

COMPATIBILITY IN YOUR OWN JOB

Have you charted your own job and style? How compatible are they? Shade in the two triangles in Exercise 7-1 and compare the results. If you have an exact match, then you should be achieving at a high level in your job. If your overall style and job are only partially compatible, then you are probably working at a lower achievement level than you could. Just how you calculate that level is our next topic of discussion.

Exercise 7-1. Assess the compatibility of your style and the requirements of your job.

Shade in triangle (a) to indicate the behavioral requirements of your job, as you did in Exercise 2-4. Then shade in triangle (b) according to your two primary managerial styles, from Exercise 3-1: allocate 3 degrees to your major style and 2 degrees to your minor style (i.e., your second style). Compare the two triangles to see how well your style matches the requirements of your job.

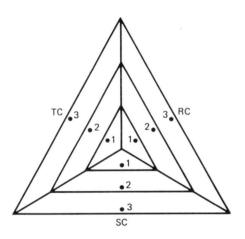

(a) **Your Job**

(See Exercise 2-4)

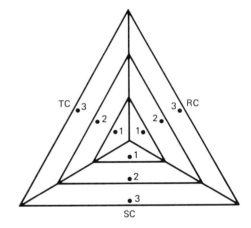

(b) **Your Style**

(See Exercise 3-1)

Since achievement results from the compatibility of overall style and job, varying degrees of compatibility should result in varying degrees of achievement. Figure 7-4 shows two managers whose styles and jobs are only partially compatible. How effective are they likely to be? Will they be high achievers or low achievers?

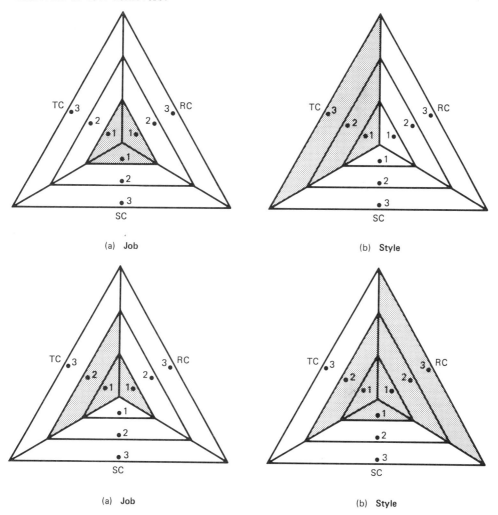

(a) Job   (b) Style

(a) Job   (b) Style

Figure 7-4.   Two Examples of Partial Compatibility between Job and Style.

In order to measure the compatibility of style and job we have developed an Achievement Index. The Achievement Index is calculated by taking the difference between Style Basis scores and Job Basis scores, *without regard for sign,* and then converting this differential score to an index score. For instance, in the first example in Figure 7-4, the manager's

118
Compatibility
and
Achievement:
Matching
Yourself
to the Job

style is described as showing 3 degrees of TC, and 0 degrees of both SC and RC. The *job* requires 1 degree each of TC, SC, and RC. Therefore, the differential score is calculated as follows:

	TC	SC	RC
Style basis	3	0	0
Job basis	1	1	1
Differential score	2 +	1 +	1 = 4

This raw differential score is then converted to an index score by using the Achievement Index Conversion Table (Table 7-1).

Table 7-1. Achievement Index Conversion Table

Differential score	9-6	5	4	3	2	1	0
Achievement score		-3	-2	-1	0	1	2	3

The manager in the example we have just been looking at has a raw differential score of 4, which converts to an Achievement Index score of -1. This indicates that he or she is likely to exhibit low-to-middling performance in this particular job. The manager is operating on the negative plane of the achievement scale shown in Figure 7-5.

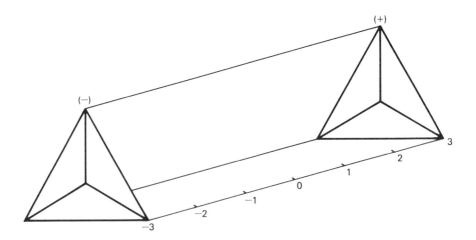

Figure 7-5. Achievement Index Scale

Now let's look at the second example in Figure 7-4. The differential score here is calculated as follows:

	TC		SC		RC		
Style basis	2		1		3		
Job basis	2		0		1		
Differential score	0	+	1	+	2	=	3

On the basis of a differential score of 3, the manager's Achievement score is 0, which puts him or her right on the neutral point of the scale. But how can that be when the job required 2 degrees of TC behavior and the manager's style matched that exactly? The major difference between the job demands and the manager's style was that the job called for only a *small* amount of relationship-centeredness, whereas the manager was heavily RC.

There is no doubt that people are very important, but, as we pointed out above, the individual who is needlessly relationship-centered just gets in the way. He or she is the Emissary, always having to be friendly, always avoiding conflict, and always concerned about being liked, no matter what. Unfortunately, when there is a job to be done, this sort of behavior is irritating to anyone who is interested in results, as it tends to be counterproductive. In this example, the manager is likely to be neither wholly effective nor wholly ineffective. When his or her behavior is task-centered, he's doing what the job requires and results will be achieved. However, it appears that this manager's major style is relationship-centered, meaning that's the style used more than any other. By definition, then, this individual will be RC when it isn't wanted or needed, and will tend to get in the way of productivity.

What was your Achievement score? Can you recognize why it turned out as it did? Do you agree with the assessment? If there was not a high degree of compatibility between your style and your job, and you are not happy with your Achievement score, what can you do about it?

HOW TO INCREASE ACHIEVEMENT

Achievement is the result of matching style and job, and when the two are incompatible, you can pursue three basic courses of action: (1) You can alter your style to fit the demands of the job; (2) you can tailor the job to match the sort of style you use most; (3) you can do a little of both. The next two chapters look at the problems of changing your style and your job demands, respectively. Both of these courses of action take work. Increasing achievement is never easy, but it is far from impossible. Many managers have been able to do it as a result of applying the principles of the M.ach One system. John Jenkins, the manager mentioned in Chapter 1, shows how it can be done. There are virtually hundreds of other people who have done the same in all types of jobs and organizations. We hope you make M.ach One work for you.

8

Behavior Adjustment: Overcoming the Peter Principle

In this book, *The Peter Principle,* Dr. Lawrence Peter argues that every manager eventually rises to his or her level of incompetence—that is, that we are eventually promoted to the point where we are unable to handle the job. Dr. Peter's book is very amusing and we have no trouble identifying people who fit the caricatures he draws. But the frightening thing is that what the book says is true in many cases. Organizations take highly successful and productive employees and promote them, only to find the employees fail dismally in the new jobs. No one can understand why. "Fred was a terrific design engineer; in fact, he was the best," they say, "but what happened to him after he was promoted to head of the design and development group? He just never seemed to fulfill his potential." Why is this such a common organizational occurrence? Can we do anything about it? And, more to the point, how can we make sure it doesn't happen to us?

Rising to one's "level of incompetence" has a great deal to do with matching style and job. As we know, different jobs often demand different types of behavior, and if the individual who moves from one to another is not able to make the necessary adjustments, performance falls off and some degree of "incompetence" develops. High achievement is the result of using the appropriate managerial style for the situation; as the match becomes less perfect, achievement levels drop. That was the topic of the last chapter, and is also the basis of the Peter Principle.

A classic example of the inability to adjust managerial style to a new job is the star salesman who is promoted to sales manager. As a salesman, he was a high achiever. He exhibited energy, enthusiasm, and drive, and his results were always excellent. In order to reward him for his success, and perhaps in the hope that his talents would rub off on some of his subordinates, he was made sales manager. And then the trouble started.

This manager is John Jenkins, mentioned in Chapter 1. He is like thousands of other salespeople who have been made sales managers on the basis of *selling* skills rather than *management* skills. The problem for this individual is that he was a good salesman because he *liked selling* and was motivated by achievement drives that the job satisfied. But when he was given a managerial position, all the fun was taken out of the job. Sales managers don't sell; they get other people to sell. They are supposed to *plan, coordinate, set strategy, delegate,* and *evaluate.* Salesmen, on the other hand, are concerned with the *implementation* of strategy, *performance, persuasion,* and the amount or *quantity* of sales. If you recall the twenty-seven critical achievement elements, you will notice that the salesman's job is described by task-centered (TC) elements, whereas the *sales manager's* job is described by situation-centered (SC) elements. Changing from successful salesman to successful sales manager means changing one's management style from Benevolent Autocrat to Professional, and that can be difficult.

STYLE AND PERSONALITY

The issue of style change is a thorny one. For a long time, psychologists maintained that one's personality is almost fixed by the age of five or six. Change was said to be exceedingly difficult, if not impossible. But are style and personality the same thing? Even though your personality is largely unchangeable, can you alter your behavior on the job?

Many management theorists and experts have maintained that personality has nothing to do with style. Style is behavior, they say, and you can behave any way you want regardless of your underlying values, attitudes, needs, and expectations. Many others find that difficult to believe. Your personality is built from your values, your attitudes, your basic needs, and your expectations in life. *Personality is defined as those relatively stable aspects of an individual that distinguish him or her from other people, and allow his or her behavior to be predicted to some degree.* If an individual's personality can aid in the prediction of his or her behavior, then the two things are, to some extent, related.

Taken to its extreme, this argument would lead us to conclude that if you can't change your personality, and personality and style are related, then you can't change your management style. But we all know of many people who have changed their styles of behavior. So where are we going wrong? We are missing two important points: (1) personality is *not* rigid and totally unchangeable; and (2) there *is* a difference between how you feel about something (your basic attitudes and values concerning it) and how you may act toward it. Let's look at both of these points.

Recent research indicates that personality is far more flexible than we thought. That is not to say that personality change is easy, because it's not. But it is possible, and it now appears to be easier than it once was, partly because of the American social and educational system that encourages self-inquiry, openness, candor, and self-awareness. We are more willing to look at ourselves and recognize our weaknesses as well as our strengths. Personality change requires that type of self-analysis. You have to know what you are before you can decide to change to something else.

The second point—that you can behave in a manner that is not in full agreement with your essential attitudes and values toward the individuals and circumstances in a situation—has also been found to be true. How many times, for example, have you been faced with a situation where you have a co-worker or subordinate whom you really don't like at all, but whom you still work with and rely on to do a good job? We've all heard the remark, "You don't have to like someone to work with him." If you had to like everyone you worked with, it might be exceedingly difficult to find a job.

The point is that personality and behavior *can* be separated. It *is* possible to be rational in a specific situation and realize that what you *want* to do is not necessarily what you *should* do. In spite of having a personality that usually causes you to shy away from challenging people, you *can* take a deep swallow and conduct a clear and objective subordinate appraisal session. In spite of desperately wanting to become personally involved in what your subordinates are doing and wanting to show them how to do it, you *can* stand back, count to ten, and delegate the responsibility to them. If you understand the demands of the situation and you understand yourself, you *can* manage the way you should to achieve results, rather than the way you would like to, to satisfy yourself. As you will recall from our discussion of management styles in Chapter 3, what separates the high-achievement, positive-style managers from the low-achievement, negative-style managers is that the former are able to respond to the demands of the job and organization, whereas the latter are totally wrapped up in their own needs.

STYLE ADJUSTMENT

We know that you *can* change your style to fit the requirements of the job, but the question of *how* this is done remains unanswered. The dynamics of the change are highly complex and the process is not completely clear, but the major factor in style adjustment certainly appears to be self-awareness. As we mentioned above, you have to understand yourself and know where you are going before you can make any clear decisions about changing your behavior.

M.ach One defines self-awareness as an understanding of one's style, strengths, weaknesses, needs, values, and goals, and of how one is perceived by other people. Having high self-awareness implies that you know how you behave in various situations, that you recognize your particular traits and quirks, and that you realize why people react to you the way they do. Everyone thinks they know these things, but research indicates quite the opposite; we tend to develop rather inaccurate pictures of ourselves.

The M.ach One system can be most helpful in increasing self-awareness because in many ways it acts like a mirror in which we can see parts of ourselves. Do some of the style descriptions in Chapter 3 ring a bell? No doubt you immediately recognized some *other* people's behavior and had a few good laughs at their expense. But what about yourself? How perceptive are you of your *own* behavior on the job? What makes you think that when your colleagues and acquaintances read the same style descriptions, they don't also chuckle as they recognize some of the things *you* do? Given the fact that other people often see things about us that we fail to see ourselves, a simple and effective mechanism for increasing self-awareness is to ask others for some feedback. (We say "simple" mechanism, but of course it is usually quite difficult to listen objectively to feedback about ourselves. We suspect that some of the things others tell us are true, but we'd rather not know for sure.)

We are not suggesting that you should either want or need feedback on how others see your personality. M.ach One is concerned about how managers behave *in their jobs*. What you need to know is how people around you perceive your *behavior* as you manage, not whether they like you or not. You want to know whether they think that the things you do, in terms of the critical achievement elements, are appropriate and will bring about high levels of achievement. Probably the first people you should go to for feedback of this type are those who work most closely with you. You can get some useful comments and ideas from your subordinates. We are all used to receiving feedback from above (and not necessarily all good) but we seldom ask those below us what they think about how things are being handled. Bear in mind that the manager's job is to have things done through others, so maybe the opinions of those "others" could be useful. (Should you decide to ask your subordinates for their feedback concerning your style and level of achievement, pay particular attention to how willingly, freely, openly, and objectively they give it to you. If they appear reluctant to discuss the topic, you might have learned something right away.) We have learned from Chapter 6 the bases for upward communication and the type of style that fosters and encourages it.

Without self-awareness, effective style adjustment can't take place. But increasing self-awareness by itself does not necessarily mean that you will reach a higher level of managerial achievement. You may understand yourself better, but the next question is, What do you want to do about it? You have to *want* to change, and you have to be willing to work hard at it. It's not easy. If it were, then the Peter Principle would be easily overcome by simply letting people know what style they needed to exhibit in their new jobs, and all would be well. The decision to adjust your style is a personal one. You have to decide whether you wish to achieve at a higher level in your job, and you have to weigh that decision against the time and effort required to make the necessary changes.

STYLE FLEXIBILITY

When we talk about the ability to adjust one's managerial behavior to fit the requirements of the job, we are really talking about an individual's style flexibility. In a changing world, flexibility is clearly a useful trait. As things change around us, we have to be able to change with them. The Chinese have a proverb that says when the wind blows very hard, the sturdy and unbending oak is uprooted and broken, but the flexible willow survives. But there are times when one has to stand firm under pressure. Sometimes change is *not* for the best.

In terms of M.ach One we define style flexibility as the ability to display behavior over at least *two* of the three basic style orientations (TC, SC, and RC). Note that we used the phrase "ability to display," since style flexibility, in M.ach One terms, refers to whether you *can* use different basic styles, not whether you *will*. Style flexibility is calculated by adding the degrees of TC, SC, and RC exhibited by a manager and converting them to a Flexibility Index made up of three ranges: High, Mid, or Low (see Table 8-1).

Table 8-1. Flexibility Conversion Table.

Degrees of basic style exhibited	0-3	4-6	7-9
Flexibility	low	mid	high

For instance, even though the manager in Figure 8-1 shows an ability to exhibit small amounts of all three basic styles, we would give him or her a low flexibility rating, the reason being that the small degree of centeredness exhibited in all styles indicates that he or she is not able to make significant changes in basic behavior. This manager can do a little of this and a little of that, but not really much of anything. Managerial jobs tend to demand that you plunge right in and commit yourself to a course of action. If you never fully commit yourself to any type of behavior but instead remain detached, you are probably more uncommitted than flexible. The manager in Figure 8-1 shows some flexibility—make no mistake about that—but he or she doesn't show a great deal of it.

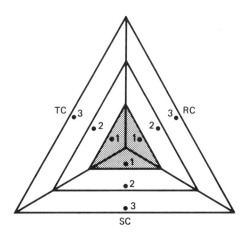

Figure 8-1. An Example of a Manager with Low Flexibility

In contrast, the manager in Figure 8-2 exhibits mid flexibility. Three degrees of SC are shown, along with one degree of each of TC and RC. This individual is essentially situation-centered, but can, if required, show a small amount of relationship-centered or task-centered behavior. One couldn't say that this individual is *highly* changeable—there are no major shifts in his or her behavior. But there is some ability to change.

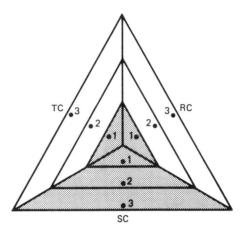

Figure 8-2.   An Example of a Manager with Mid Flexibility

And finally, Figure 8-3 shows an example of a manager with high flexibility—three degrees of TC, one of SC, and three of RC.

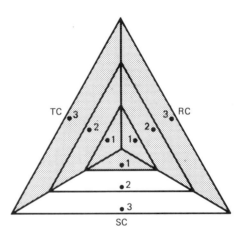

Figure 8-3.   An Example of a Manager with High Flexibility

Is Flexibility Good or Bad?

When your job demands that you use a variety of styles, or when it changes so that your old style is no longer appropriate, then flexibility is clearly an asset. The ability to adjust your behavior in these types of situations will get you through many problems. But let's be careful about how we approach this matter of change. It isn't always a good idea to "go with the flow." There are times when change is wrong, when doing something the old way is best rather than giving in to pressure to try the latest "in" thing.

There is no doubt that individuals who can command a variety of different styles in different situations have a definite advantage over their fellow managers. But how they use that flexibility is another matter. Do they make the right move at the right time, changing their style when the situation requires it, or do they change their behavior at the wrong time and for the wrong reasons? Is style adjustment made in order to increase managerial achievement over the long run, or is it just aimed at relieving some of the short-term pressures the manager is feeling at the moment? There is a great difference between changing your style because you should in order to get better results, and changing it to reduce pressure on you so that you will *feel* better. Remember, the bottom line is always achievement.

There are certainly times when you should *not* change your managerial style. Strong managers have the ability to stand pat when they know they are doing the right thing. Some jobs are far from popular, and the people who have to perform them receive many complaints. An example is the job of internal auditor. Nobody likes the internal auditor questioning their actions and decisions, and telling them they aren't doing things properly. However, that's his job—he is there to make sure that the proper procedures are followed, and that financial data are reported correctly. The person performing this job is often accused of not giving a damn about people. However, an internal auditor is responsible for seeing that things are done exactly as they're supposed to be, and he cannot afford to be too concerned with whether it upsets people. His behavior outside the job may be quite different, but on the job itself, friendships are not a major priority.

When you face a situation in which you have to produce, and produce fast, you need to adopt a task-centered approach. This may generate short-term frustrations among your employees, and you may feel the pressure for a more relationship-centered orientation. The question you have to ask is, If I alter my behavior, will I still be able to achieve the production level that is needed? The issue is not whether you will feel better, but whether the desired results will occur.

By the same token, if the situation requires that you develop strong, capable subordinates who feel a high degree of loyalty to the job and organization, this entails an esssentially relationship-centered approach, and you will need to resist the temptation take full control over projects when they appear to be getting into difficulty. In the short term, such an approach may make it easier for you to get the job done, but it won't produce the result you want or need in the long run. Watching subordinates struggle through something you can do well yourself isn't easy, but sometimes it has to be done—you want *them* to be able to do the job. Style *stability* is essential in these situations.

The Neutral Management Styles and Flexibility

We said earlier that the positive management styles reflected behavior that is essentially organization-oriented, whereas the negative styles are concerned with behavior that is influenced largely by personality. The high-achievement manager is able to adjust his or her style to the demands of the job, whereas the low achiever is locked into a set pattern, regardless of the circumstances. But what about managers whose styles fall on the neutral plane? What can we say about them?

All of the neutral styles (Technocrat, Bureaucrat, and Diplomat) show a marked tendency to alter their behavior inappropriately. The main reason for the variabiity in achievement levels of managers who use these styles is that all these styles proceed from a sense of *personal compromise*. That is, the Technocrat is torn between a love for the technology and the need to work with other people to get things done; the Bureaucrat is torn between a love for order and system and the vagaries of the individuals with whom he has to work; and the Diplomat is torn between the love of personal aggrandizement and the demands of others that they be rewarded, too. In each of these cases, the manager is faced with strong demands, both of a *personal* nature and an *organizational* nature, and has a difficult time deciding which one to give in to. The result is that he or she tends to do the wrong thing at the wrong time—behavioral flexibility occurs when it is not needed.

We are all faced with this type of dilemma from time to time. Just how much should we do for the organization and how much should we do for ourselves? If we give our all, devote our entire lives to the organization, what will we receive in return? The ever-present fear is that it might be just a gold watch and a handshake, and so we want to make sure that we keep an eye out for ourselves. On the other hand, any conscientious manager knows that if you don't care enough about the organization, you can't do much of a job. You *have* to care. You have to feel some sense of ownership and loyalty. But you also have to feel that the loyalty will be recognized and rewarded. What you need to do is find a way to achieve your own goals and those of the organization simultaneously. When you achieve your goals and objectives by doing what the organization needs to have done, everybody wins.

THE RISKS OF STYLE ADJUSTMENT

Style adjustment is possible, but like all change, it involves some degree of risk. For one thing, it might not work; you might not be able to operate in the new style that well (at least to start with), and results may fall off. Nobody wants to fail, and there is a danger that if you interrupt a relatively successful pattern of behavior—presumably the one that got you to where you are now—you might lose what you have already achieved. We have all developed our management styles over time, and what we are doing at present is most likely what has proven to be successful for us in the past. Think back to a situation in which you were given something completely new and different to do. How did you approach it? Most likely you tried some things that you had done in other situations. It is a natural tendency to start off doing what we are familiar with and have been relatively successful doing in the past. However, old patterns of behavior may not work in a new situation. Yet before we can learn *new* behavior, we have to *un*learn the old behavior.

What happens when learned behavior becomes inappropriate over time is well illustrated by an experiment sometimes conducted with fish. The experimenter places a large fish in one half of a glass tank and a number of small minnows in the other half. The divider is transparent colorless glass so that the big fish can see the little minnows clearly. Since obviously big fish have grown up by eating little fish, the big fish in the tank will of course attempt to eat some of the minnows. Unfortunately for the fish, each time he strikes at a minnow, he bumps his head against the glass. After repeated bumps, the big fish begins to get the message: "Every time I try to eat a minnow, something socks me on the nose. If I want to stop getting socked on the nose, I'd better stop trying to eat the minnows." Eventually the big fish stops striking at the minnows completely. In fact, even when the dividing partition is removed and the minnows swim all around him, the fish will not make any moves toward them. The fish has learned to behave differently, and, for a fish, inappropriately.

In this experiment, the fish has learned to behave inappropriately because big fish make their living by eating little fish. He has actually been taught to stop doing the very thing on which his entire life depends! By pulling out the dividing pane of glass the fish is told, "Go ahead and eat the minnows. All is forgiven." But he is much too smart to fall for that one, because he remembers all those socks on the nose. He will starve to death unless he has become accustomed to some other form of food.

People in organizations often behave like the fish in the tank. Management tells employees not to do something, and it only takes them a short time to learn that the forbidden behavior results in a sock in the nose. Then, when management decides that what was once taboo is now acceptable, they can't understand why people won't change. The organization has taught its members that a certain behavior is inappropriate and it is now faced with the long and arduous task of getting them to unlearn it.

When you decide to change your style, you are like the experimenter who removed the glass pane. Your subordinates have learned how to react to you and how you want them to behave, and you may be disappointed when you suddenly make a basic change and expect them to respond positively to it. Style change often has to be a slow process. It requires patience and a great deal of *un*learning both on your part and on the part of the people you work with. Try to remember that, and don't get frustrated when everything doesn't fall into place as soon as you make the decision to change your style.

9

Tailoring Your Job
for a Styl(ish) Fit

If you find that there is a poor match between your job demands and your style, must you face the difficult prospect of altering your managerial behavior? Is there no other way to solve the problem? Does high achievement rest on the continued ability to adjust style to each different job you encounter during your career? If style change was the only available alternative, managerial life would be a series of traumas for most of us. Fortunately, there is another way.

ALTERING YOUR JOB TO MATCH YOUR STYLE

Managers seldom think of altering their jobs in order to increase achievement. We tend to take the job as given—it's there and we have to do it. The organization chart becomes written in stone, and it takes a major effort by the planning people or a consultant to change it. Job descriptions tend to remain static, either because the people who write them lose interest once they're completed, or the individuals doing the jobs pay little attention to the job description and simply do what has to be done. Managerial jobs do not receive the attention, in terms of design and change, that they deserve.

As every practicing manager knows, however, in reality a job as it is performed is constantly changing. Duties are added, combined, altered, and even (on rare occasions) deleted. These changes tend to occur subtly, often rapidly, and with dismal regularity. Because of this constant change, managers may lose a clear understanding of their jobs. Responsibilities, goals, objectives, and authority all tend to become somewhat blurred, and in a short time the job becomes very different from what it was originally. This is why many mismatches occur, and why many managers seem to achieve less and less over time.

At this point you're probably thinking, "How on earth can I change my job? That's decided by someone above me, and I certainly can't admit that I'm not able to handle things as they are." Well, altering your job to fit your strengths is easier than you think. You don't have to confess to an inability to cope, and you don't have to have formal changes recorded in quintuplicate and authorized by three officers of the company. This chapter discusses a number of ways of tailoring your job to your style and gives examples of how actual managers have done so successfully.

135

Eliminate What's Unimportant

A point we've made repeatedly throughout the book is that in order to achieve the maximum in a job, you have to establish priorities. You have to know what's critical, what's important, and what's icing on the cake. Your job, then, comprises activities of various degrees of importance, plus a number of unimportant activities that lead to virtually nothing by way of results. One of the easiest ways of altering your job is to focus only on the top priorities and stop doing things that are not important.

Ask yourself why you attend certain meetings, why you write certain memos, or reply to letters within a day, or read everything that comes across your desk. If you simply stopped doing some of these things, what would happen? Would there be any change in job results? You will probably find that when you stop doing things you don't do well, or things that take up too much of your valuable time, your achievement increases.

Learn to Delegate

Another solution to a mismatch between management style and the requirements of the job is to concentrate your efforts on what is most important and what you do well, and call on the resources of the organization to provide support in other areas. Much of the success of this strategy, of course, depends on whether you are capable of handling the essential parts of your job successfully. If the most important part of the job requires relationship-centered behavior and that is definitely your weakest suit, then you are clearly in the wrong job. However, unless you have been placed in a position that is totally unsuited to you, chances are that the critical parts of the job are well within your reach.

By focusing on the critical aspect of the job and recognizing that other duties were too important to be overlooked or mishandled, the manager in the following example used delegation as a way to utilize his major strengths and still see that those responsibilities at which he was not particularly adept were carried out.

The research manager in a large pharmaceutical firm diagnosed his job and his style as shown in Figure 9-1. Essentially, the job required a relationship-centered style, with some situation-centeredness. The manager saw himself as being very good at dealing with people and relating to them, and he was able to keep his staff of researchers happy, committed, and motivated. However, when it came to handling the administrative details involved in budgeting, planning, and coordinating the activities of the lab, he was much less effective.

Although the researchers themselves were pleased with the way the lab was run—they were by and large left alone to do what they wanted, within the confines of the budget and the goals of the program—top management was less happy. It felt that there was inadequate financial control, that reports were slow in being generated, and that in general the lab was running

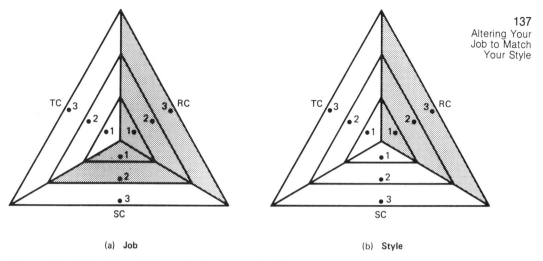

(a) Job   (b) Style

Figure 9-1. The Job and Style of a Pharmaceutical Company's Research Manager

without any significant direction. The research manager knew he was a poor administrator. He just couldn't work up much interest in figures, reports, schedules, plans, and the details of presentations. He was a researcher at heart, and he felt close to the problems and concerns of the research staff. But he also knew that if he didn't maintain control over the lab and keep top management in close touch with what was going on in the various programs, he simply would not achieve what was expected of him.

He knew that it would be next to impossible for him to alter his style. His entire training and career to date had been built around his research capabilities and his skill in working with people and getting them to perform well, and these were also the top priorities of his job. But the administrative side of his job was where the problems were arising, and where he felt he didn't have the skills, or the inclination, to improve. His solution was to hire an assistant to monitor budgets, remind project heads to submit progress reports, and handle minor administrative details such as ordering supplies, allocating support staff, arranging travel, and so on. In this way the manager could continue to concentrate only on what was critically important—and on what he was good at.

Many managers resist delegating even the most minor responsibilities of their job to others, for fear of losing control or becoming out of touch in areas that effect their day-to-day operations. The following example shows how one such manager found that through delegation he was actually in *better* control of the truly important elements of his job.

The chairman and chief executive officer of an electric utility firm was a man with unbounded energy. He prided himself on being in close touch with every aspect of the company, and on being highly accessible to the consumers of his firm's services. Any individual could call the head office and reach the chairman on the telephone. Even though many of these calls were simply to report power outages, the chairman usually spent a few minutes in friendly conversation with callers and felt that this time was well spent in "public relations."

Problems arose when the executive committee found itself faced with critical strategic decisions concerning the building of new generating facilities, changeovers to alternate forms of generating fuels, and a possible corporate merger. Because these questions were of an all-encompassing nature, large blocks of time were necessary to discuss them fully. However, the chairman was constantly besieged with calls and letters that made long meetings almost impossible. It was only when the situation became highly charged with frustration on the part of the rest of the executives that he was made to realize that his "open" style had to change. The job of handling telephone calls and writing letters to customers was delegated to a senior secretary, the desk was taken from the his office and replaced with easy chairs and coffee tables, and his day was spent meeting with key members of the corporate team and making strategic decisions.

By simply delegating to someone else the minor jobs of taking routine telephone calls and responding to routine letters, the chairman's achievement level was increased noticeably. His change in behavior was explained to customers by the secretary who handled the calls and letters. She noted that he was no longer able to personally respond to individual callers, but that he kept a close eye on the correspondence and the calls and maintained a high interest in them. Customers were just as happy to be talking to someone in the chairman's office. Meanwhile, the chairman no longer felt compelled to take the calls because they weren't relayed to his office; he wasn't able to draft letters because he no longer retained a desk; and his office was set up conveniently for meetings, which were the top priority anyway. He remained at the center of the action, kept his finger on the pulse of the decisions, and was able to infuse the other senior executives with his drive and energy. In short, by delegating to someone else the items of questionable priority in his job he was able to focus his attention where it was needed, and to achieve some important results for the corporation.

Once again, we see that the tailoring process can be relatively simple. If there is a part of your job that you don't do well, or that is taking an inordinate amount of your time and keeping you away from more important activities, delegate it to someone else. If your weak suit is dealing with people, find someone to handle the people-related activities. If you're taking too much time checking on production floor activities, find someone else to check them for you. If finances are your weak point, enlist the aid of someone who is strong in that area. Most organizations are filled with people who can easily take on some additional responsibility, so use them.

Eliminate the things that do not produce critical results for you by finding a subordinate to handle them. Delegation is constantly preached, but seldom practiced. Remember that a manager's job is to manage the work of others, so don't fall into the trap of trying to do everything yourself.

Trade Parts of the Job

Most organizations are structured in work units of varying size. An organization can be thought of as a set of interlocking work units, as shown in Figure 9-2, with each of the units having the responsibility to do a certain job and to achieve certain results. Within these work groups, each individual has a specific job and specific goals. The critical thing, from the manager's point of view, is not so much whether each individual within the group achieves all these goals, but whether the unit as a whole achieves its objectives. The manager of the unit is rewarded for the *unit's* performance and can balance the poor performance of one individual with the superior performance of another. What this means is that subordinates can trade parts of their jobs as long as the overall job is done. The following example shows how one manager successfully applied this strategy.

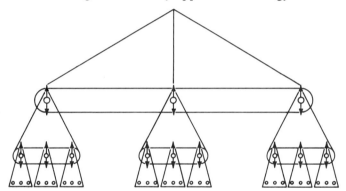

Figure 9-2. Interlocking Units within an Organization

The manager of the wage and salary administration unit within the personnel department of a large international firm was highly intelligent and hard-working, and extremely competent in compiling and analyzing data, processing pay revision applications, and generally administrating the section's files and paperwork. However, when she had to deal face-to-face with individual heads of departments to explain the ratings given their people and the compensation levels decided on for each position, she ran into problems. She thought she had done her work properly, given the available data and the company's policy guidelines for wage and salary levels, and that there was no need for any further discussion of the matter. She simply explained why certain decisions had been made and had no subsequent interest in the arguments of the people involved, unless they were based on additional raw data that she and her staff had not had to begin with.

The department heads she interacted with found her annoying, and so a great deal of animosity built up toward the personnel department in general. The manager knew there was a problem, but she didn't want to change the way she did her job because she thought that she was correct and that department managers should be mature enough to accept the facts of organizational life, one of which was the pay scale and the system on which it was calculated. That department heads were *not* able to do so irked her, but she realized that they had to be accommodated in some fashion.

The solution to the problem involved a trade with the head of the labor negotiation section. The wage and salary manager agreed to do some statistical compilation and analysis for the negotiation section, and its head took on the job of meeting with department heads to discuss compensation problems. The head negotiator had considerable interpersonal skills and was able to get managers to accept compensation packages with relative ease. He was also able to have some plans altered despite strong objections from department heads. On the other hand, the negotiating unit was supplied with much sharper analyses of data on which to base their own work, and the head of the negotiation unit felt that the trade with the wage and salary unit was more than fair.

Very often we can do most of our job well, but we stumble on the small part that we are unsuited for. Unfortunately, the tiny portion of the job that we do poorly often seems to be much more noticeable than the large portion that we do well. One remedy to this situation is to trade the part of your job that you don't do well, or that you don't like, with someone else. If both of you concentrate on what you do well, the team as a whole benefits. That's all that matters in the end. If the unit does its job and everyone in it seems pleased with the way the work is divided, much of the problem can be solved. Certainly, as far as performance evaluation and reward are concerned, you should have the approval of your boss, and you should at some juncture go through the required paperwork changes, if that is important in your organization. But don't rule out the alternative of trading parts of your job. It's a method that has a high rate of success, and it is a relatively quick means of allowing you to concentrate on what you do best.

Share Parts of the Job

Achievement can also be hindered by the desire to keep all the credit for it oneself. But if you are mainly interested in getting things done and you don't particularly mind who is rewarded for it, individual effort will become less important and shared contribution more effective. You'd be amazed at how much you can accomplish if you don't mind someone else getting the credit. Consider the following example:

Profits in an electronics component firm were lagging because of difficulties in coordinating production and delivery from several plants with sales in many different areas. Although plant *A* was supposed to serve its surrounding geographical area by supplying the product to the salesforce in area *A*, and plants *B* and *C* were supposed to do the same for their areas, sometimes sales and production levels in a specific geographical region became unbalanced, and the product had to be brought in or shipped out from another area to meet these needs. The production people blamed marketing for the problems, while the marketing department blamed production. The only party that didn't know who to blame was the customer, who too often simply took his business elsewhere when unable to receive delivery of needed components.

The resolution of the problem lay in a sharing of the overall objective of profit and cash flow for the firm. The marketing and production managers got together and agreed to take a *shared* responsibility for sales. Each one agreed that it was not helpful to sell what wasn't available, or to produce what wasn't selling, and that they would have to bear the burden of results jointly. Once that was agreed, both departments could get on with what they did best and did not have to worry about, or interfere with, what they knew much less about.

However, sharing responsibility does have a potential problem: both parties must be committed to holding up their end of the bargain. Too often, shared responsibility becomes an excuse for failing to achieve objectives—it is always the other person's fault. If you are committed to sharing responsibility for a goal or product, and you are sincere in making the required effort to ensure its achievement, how can you ensure that the other party will think and act the same way? The answer becomes clear when you stand back and think of why *you're* so keen on the idea; you stand to gain in some way from achieving the goal. The job is important to you, and you think that accomplishing it would be good both for you and the organization. But what about the other party to this "shared" deal? What does he or she think about it? To get commitment from the other party, you must make sure that they find the outcome beneficial to *them* as well. *Both* sides have to benefit, and, what is just as important, both sides have to *see* that they're going to benefit. The following example illustrates this point.

Two senior executives in a major petroleum company in Europe simply could not agree over a critical area of their respective jobs. Manager *A* was responsible for profits generated by the company's service stations. Since the profit margin on gasoline and associated petroleum products was relatively low, the manager introduced a line of prepared food and beverage products that were marketed to motorists when they stopped to fill up. The line was particularly successful in service stations that were located next to motels also owned and operated by the company. The service stations in these locations built grassed picnic areas with tables, benches, and swings for children. Weary motorists could then fill up with gasoline, and at the same time purchase food and drinks for a picnic meal that they could consume in a pleasant setting.

The problem arose with manager *B*, who was responsible for the company's motel chain. He, too, was faced with lower revenues and margins than he would have liked, and it irked him to see potential customers who might have used his dining rooms and coffee shops make their purchases from the service stations. He argued that food and beverages were his responsibility and his domain, and that the petroleum products end of the business should stay within its own boundaries. Each customer who purchased food or drink from the service station represented lost revenue for the hotel operations.

In this situation, both managers *A* and *B* were ultimately held responsible for profitability in their own areas, while the company was concerned about the total picture. How could responsibility for *overall* profit be shared equitably? The conflict eventually escalated between them to the point where they stopped talking to one another.

The dispute was finally resolved when the managing director intervened and worked out a mutually satisfactory formula for assessing performance in each of the divisions. The result of the agreed solution was that both parties felt they benefited. Both were happy with the deal, and both were committed to making it work.

Sometimes, a mutually satisfactory agreement stems from a reworking of the reward system, as in the above example. Without a revision of the existing system, shared responsibilities can often result in abdication of responsibility by one or more parties, and an overload of responsibility on some others.

Although jobs can be changed by sharing parts of them with others, keep in mind that objectives may not be achieved if the other party to the sharing does not hold up his or her end of the bargain. The key to success is to make sure that both you and the other party stand to benefit equally, and that you both clearly understand this. Such a change may require a superior's approval of both the sharing and the division of rewards.

Change the System

Some jobs fall on your shoulders simply because the system routes them your way. They either don't have to be done by you, or else they don't have to be done in a particular way by you. If they happen to include things that you don't do well, one means of increasing your achievement is to alter the system. Major changes, of course, are often impossible, but small changes can have a big effect on your job, as shown in the following example:

The head of a community service agency received all the guidelines and procedure recommendations of the national headquarters, as well as information on government funding for the local agency. She was expected to call meetings of the advisory board to present them with this information and to decide on policy for the agency. Because she was the individual who received the data, she also prepared the agenda and chaired the meetings. The problem was that two powerful and vocal members of the advisory board usually made the meetings the ground for fierce arguments. The job of chairperson grew increasingly difficult because each of the two warring individuals attacked the chair whenever their own points of view weren't accepted.

The head of the agency solved the problem by alternately routing monthly data to one and then the other of the two argumentative individuals, who then became responsible for chairing the monthly meeting. The arguments abated somewhat because each realized that he would have to chair the next meeting, and whatever he gave out, he could be sure to get back when his own time came to act as chairperson. The discussion moved away from personal attacks and irresponsible accusations, and the agency head found the board more able and willing to engage the central issues facing them.

The system needs people to do certain things, but often it need not be you. If you can get the job done and have the demands of the system met without having to do things that you don't or can't handle well, you may be able to achieve more in other areas of your job. Probably the simplest example of this we've seen is the following:

An energetic and talented manager in a large but high-growth company found that a significant amount of his time was being taken up with analysis of market data. The analysis was done weekly as information came in from the field, and the results were used at regular Tuesday meetings of the marketing group. The data were sent in to head office on Friday, received Monday morning, and the analysis had to be completed by Tuesday afternoon. The manager found that he spent a minimum of a half day each week preparing his analysis. He felt that with the company growing so rapidly and with new markets being found and entered constantly, his time would be better spent elsewhere.

In conversation at a social gathering, he lamented this aspect of his job and remarked how much he disliked it. A woman in the group hit on the solution with a casual comment: "Why don't you get your computer to analyze the information?"—a simple solution to an annoying problem! Since the data always arrived in the same form, it was relatively easy for the computer to do the same analysis that the manager had formerly done by hand. Summary charts, graphics, and so on were easily generated by the machine once it was decided what the manager wanted. Thus he had his half day free to get on with what he considered work of major priority. (We'd like to tell you that he fell in love with the brilliant woman who gave him this suggestion and the two of them lived happily ever after, but the truth is, she was his mother.)

THE JOB CONSENSUS MEETING

Most managerial and supervisory jobs are interactive. That is, the work is carried out through interaction with others—superiors, co-workers, or subordinates. Often what you perceive as your job is not the same as what others see. They may think you do some things which are unnecessary or unimportant, or perhaps that you have an unclear picture of your job as a whole. You can simply ask others for their opinions, but you will probably learn more if you can arrange a meeting of your entire work group. Discussion at the meeting should be devoted entirely to the question of who should do what, and the relative importance of various activities and objectives. If everyone can agree on what they're supposed to be doing, what their major priorities are, and where they should be focusing time and attention, you will almost certainly increase achievement.

A job consensus meeting need only take a day. Each individual invited to the meeting should spend some time in advance analyzing his or her own job and identifying the highly important and less important areas in it. Participants should also put some thought into the overall goals of the work unit and how they can best be achieved. The meeting should begin by trying to reach a consensus on the unit's overall goals and priorities, then each individual's job should be discussed in terms of how it can best contribute to the attainment of those objectives. The focus should be on responsibilities and outputs rather than on activities. It is less important to decide on *how* something is to be done than it is to decide on *what* should be done.

SUMMARY

Changing the dimensions of a job is not as difficult as it may appear on the surface. Managers who simply shrug and say they can't change anything are also telling you something: they aren't interested in achieving more. Of course, the higher you are in your organization, the more leeway you have in changing the way your job is done; but even at the lowest levels, it's unusual for a job to have *no* flexibility. The changes that need to be made are sometimes very small, but it's like trying to run with a stone in your shoe—taking the stone out is simple, but running at your best without removing it is exceedingly difficult.

Look at your job closely. Consider each of the Critical Achievement Elements and ask yourself if there are some that you don't manage easily or well. If there are, then you must try to find a way to change them. Either you have to alter your style in some manner, or else you have to try to alter the way the job is done so that you can focus your time and energy on the things at which you excel, and minimize the effort spent on things you do less well. There is no escaping the fact that we all have to do some things we don't particularly like. However, if you want to achieve high levels of results in your job, you should focus as much of your talent as possible on potential high payoff areas. Play on strengths and discard weaknesses.

10

The Western Response to Japanese Management

Many recent books, articles, and television shows have said that Japanese managers are better than their western counterparts. They cite our relatively poor productivity figures (since World War II our productivity has risen only 25 percent as rapidly as Japan's), and they decry the loss to the Japanese of major industries such as the motorcycle and television industries that were once "owned" by the western nations. The message is that the Japanese know something we don't know, that they're doing something we aren't doing and that we'd better begin to copy them fast before they take away the automobile and computer businesses that they now seem to be threatening so ominously.

If the Japanese have all the answers, why hasn't this book, which purports to provide a method for increasing managerial achievement, discussed what they're doing and what we should be doing to copy them? Are we missing the boat somehow? Are the techniques and approaches talked about in the previous nine chapters less effective than Japanese methods? The answer is definitely no, and there are a number of good reasons why—reasons that the books, articles, and TV shows have overlooked in the panic that seems to have hit us in the face of the Japanese "invasion."

WHY THE JAPANESE DON'T HAVE ALL THE ANSWERS

Many Japanese companies setting up shop in North America or Europe are using a number of their management techniques with great success. Although they have modified the basic approach somewhat to suit the host country's culture, these firms are run in a very "Japanese" way. Among the large Japanese companies in the United States are Mitsui, the Bank of Tokyo, Fujitsu, Sony, Matsushita, Sanyo, and Nissan. The Japanese, contrary to what we may be told, haven't mounted an "invasion" of our territory. Only one of these companies, Mitsui—which is in the aluminum industry through its 45 percent ownership of Alumax—is among the fifty largest foreign investors in the United States. But, invasion or not, Japanese companies have been, and are, very successful in the West.

When we look at foreign companies moving into Japan, however, the picture is quite different. Firms there don't take western methods and transplant them to Japan; they *all* manage their operations in the Japanese fashion. Even large companies like IBM and McDonald's, both of whom have been highly successful in Japan, leave management in the hands of the

Japanese and run their companies using Japanese methods. Why is this so? Does it mean that there is only one successful way to manage, and that it happens to be the way the Japanese do it? Why can the Japanese implement their practices so easily, while we can't? Have we been doing everything wrong?

The answer lies in the differences between the cultures of Japan and the West, particularly in Japan's *homogeneity* versus the West's *heterogeneity*. Japan has a tightly knit culture. The country has never been invaded in recorded history and has centuries-long traditions and customs that are deeply ingrained in its society. The culture is highly homogeneous and essentially classless; over 90 percent of Japanese define themselves as "middle class." They are also highly group-oriented, and have no sense of identity outside the group. Their lives revolve around their various relationships with family, company, community, and nation. This phenomenon has been described by the noted scholar and consultant on Japan Geoffrey Bownas as being like living within a nest of "lobster pots"—each group is part of a larger group, and once in, never out. All Japanese, then, are part of a set of groups to which they owe, and deliver, a high degree of loyalty. Mobility between groups is almost nonexistent. A Japanese manager who chooses to switch from a company in one industrial group to another completely different firm in a different group can expect to suffer a 40 percent cut in salary. However, not only is the prospect of a huge loss of income daunting, but this manager would not be welcome in the second company and would have little chance of success or happiness there.

Japan is a society in which all the people hold similar values. Certainly there is disagreement and discussion, but life overall is highly ordered, disciplined, and based on deeply and strongly held traditional values, many of which date back to the Tokugawa period of the 1600's and before. Although Confucianism has had its ups and downs in Japan, its essential values of respect and affection between father and son, respect and loyalty between master and servant, and trust between friends remain deeply entrenched in the society. In addition, the traditional military code of the samurai, the Bushido, which stressed absolute loyalty to one's lord, is still manifested in many ways. These various behavioral codes are enforced by strong group pressure: failure to conform results in ostracism, and, given the nature of Japanese society, that would be unbearable. The Japanese have a long history of strong group identity; they see the group as the main source of security and prosperity in life, and their moral values support deep and unquestioning loyalty to it. There is no identity outside the group, as is evident from the way Japanese workers describe themselves. They talk in terms of their company affiliations rather than their job titles or professions—that is "I am a Matsushita man," rather than "I'm an engineer," or "I'm in marketing."

You can see, just from that brief description of their culture, that the Japanese follow very different rules than we do, and that these rules are not very flexible. They have played by them for centuries, and they aren't about to change now. Their culture is far more homogeneous than ours and more resistant to change.

On the other hand, North Americans have a somewhat diverse and loosely knit cultural fabric. Our history is relatively short. Our population is made up of people from a wide variety of cultural backgrounds, and we value individual freedom highly. Essentially, everyone can do his or her own thing, and there's room for tremendous differences. We can, and do, assimilate aspects of every culture—just the opposite of Japan. And that's why we're able to use many of their methods while they find most of ours unacceptable.

The Japanese have *some* answers to managerial problems, and certainly we should pay attention to their methods, but bear in mind that effective management depends a great deal on the culture. The question is, do the main elements of Japanese management fit our western culture? There seems to be a consensus that these elements work very well in Japan, and in the light of that country's successes on the world scene, we should see what can be immediately transferred to our organizations. We can't afford to ignore successful practices purely because of national pride. If they work well, let's swallow our pride and give them a try.

In order to discuss and evaluate the merits of the Japanese approach to business as opposed to ours, we need to look more closely at some basic issues—particularly the differences between the cultures and the differences in management methods. These have to be understood before an opinion can be formed as to the merits of one side or the other.

FUNDAMENTAL ISSUES OF WESTERN MANAGEMENT

What we do, in a general sense, reflects our basic values, ideals, and beliefs. We manage our organizations the way we do because we think it's the right way. Right and wrong are difficult concepts to define; essentially they represent some sort of collective agreement within a given society. We agree, for example, that it is wrong to use child labor, but is it wrong to employ only females, or only whites? Or is it wrong to terminate employment for people over age fifty-five? We can only make these judgments on the basis of society's view of these issues. The Japanese have no difficulty accommodating sexist and racist policies, and employment generally ends at fifty-five. Who is right, and who is wrong? In our culture, we are right, and they are wrong, but in their culture, it is the other way around.

Four basic differences stand out in our approach to management versus that of the Japanese: The differences arise from these two society's basic values and beliefs about life and the way it should be lived. These beliefs and values show through in the way we handle both our personal lives and our organizational lives. Let's examine these differences in more detail.

- Individualism vs. Group-centeredness
- Independence vs. Control
- Specialization vs. Generalization
- Equality of Opportunity vs. Hierachical Stratification

Individualism vs. Group-Centeredness

As noted earlier, in Japan the group is everything. There is no life outside a group. The Japanese first encounter the strong bonds of the family, then the community, then the organization and the work group within it, and then the nation. For centuries, the Japanese have had to depend on one another. Japan is a small country, with little useful land. Until comparatively recently, travel was next to impossible. In order to live harmoniously in close circumstances, complex and highly regulated patterns of interpersonal relationships were developed, one of the more significant being the concept of On, or benevolence, whereby individuals higher in the social hierarchy were bound to extend favors to those below them, and the recipients of these favors were *obligated* to return them. Thus a system arose in which virtually everyone was placed in a position of "owing" something to someone else. This results in strong bonds with many people, and constantly reinforces the belief that life exists only within a group—the individual relies on the group, and vice versa.

We in the West have a different view of life. We believe that "the Lord helps those that help themselves." Crudely put, this is the Protestant work ethic (a concept that is certainly not restricted to Protestants). We believe in individual effort, and when things become difficult, whom do we turn to? Ourselves. "When the going gets tough, the tough get going" is a favorite motto of many, and we lionize the individuals who live by it. Who are our great heroes? They are all individuals who can take the bit in their teeth and who, through determination and application, can wrest success out of difficult situations. We love the underdog because he or she has to face the greatest difficulty and has to work harder to overcome it. And we love individual heroes more than teams, groups, or organizations.

Western individuality and Japanese group-centeredness are reflected in the way each society handles difficult situations. The Japanese rely on the group to make important decisions and to take action. The individual is merely an instrument of the group and does not succeed purely on his own merits. We, however, rely on the individual. We expect the star quarterback to pull the game out of the fire at the last minute. We hail the individual astronauts rather than the thousands of support people who work in the space program. We expect great deeds from great individuals and are shocked and disappointed when they are unable to rise to the occasion. All of Mudville is let down when the mighty Casey strikes out.

Our discussion of achievement throughout this book has referred primarily to individual achievement. We're certainly not a society of loners, but when we think of achieving and getting ahead, we are thinking about ourselves as individuals, not some group of which we are a part. Certainly we all have group affiliations—family, club, union, community, team, and the like—and we attempt to help the other members achieve goals. But one of the dominant characteristics of the high achiever, as you know, is the desire to be able to claim individual responsibility for success. The achiever finds the taste of victory sweeter when he or she has done it alone. When success is the result of the actions of others, we don't enjoy it as much.

We're not all egocentrics, but on the scale between individualism and group-centeredness, most of us lean toward the individualistic end.

Independence vs. Control

Ours is also a society in which we do not gladly accept authority. People came to North America originally because they wanted to escape the authoritarian systems under which they lived. They came here to be independent, to get on with their own business in their own way, with the minimum of interference. We value freedom above all. We may make the wrong choices, but we desperately want to have the freedom to be able to make them. The thought of being locked in a single organization for a lifetime is unattractive to most people in North America. Even when they stay in a single company during their entire working lives, individuals like to think they could change if they wished to.

Perhaps it's a weakness, but most individuals in our culture want a great deal of freedom in their lives. The authors have asked just short of a thousand managerial and nonmanagerial people from private and public organizations in North America and Europe, how much separation exists between their lives in the organization and their private lives. Almost all the respondents said that they try to draw a clear line between job and private life. Subsequent interviews have shown that many of them have not drawn the line clearly, but the fact that they *want* to do so is important. The Japanese see their jobs as an integral part of their lives, and their organizations as extensions of the "family." Their social lives center on the people in the organization, and even their community status may depend on how they are perceived to be doing in their organizations.

Americans certainly like to belong to groups and organizations, but these have little to do with work in a formal sense. Service clubs, associations, community groups, and churches take up much of our time, but we like to think we are free to join or to leave any of these groups at any time. As soon as the demands of an organization become excessive, we begin to think of how to break away. We don't like to be controlled by others. Most of us are not happy in a regimented, structured, disciplined situation—especially if it's all-encompassing and there is no chance to voice individual complaints or opinions. The Japanese, on the other hand, quite happily accept a great number of "rules." They are more "disciplined" and more willing to accept controls and restrictions on activity. That outlook leads to a different approach to running an organization. But remember what the fourth of July is called in the United States—it's certainly not "Group Cooperation Day." We much prefer independence to control, and our organizations and management methods reflect it.

Specialization vs. Generalization

The Japanese approach to career development is different from that of most western organizations. The Japanese manager experiences constant job rotation, moving from function to function, department to department, and even company to company (within a group). The aim is to develop managers who have a broad grasp of organizational problems from a variety of perspectives. The Japanese manager is a generalist rather than a specialist.

Western managers, in general, tend to move upward within specific functions. Studies indicate that individuals who reach the top echelons in their organizations have typically spent almost all their careers in one function, with perhaps a brief sojourn in one other. Our business culture seems to emphasize "technical" expertise in specific areas.

There are advantages and disadvantages to both systems. The Japanese system produces well-rounded managers who can take a wide view of organizational issues, and who are perhaps better able to coordinate diverse functions in order to focus on major problems. The generalist approach fits with the practice of making most decisions by consensus. Everyone in the group understands the problem in a wider sense, and there tends to be more common ground on which to reach an agreement. Information flows more easily because managers understand one another better. Specialists, on the other hand, often find it difficult to communicate with one another effectively, simply because they see things differently and are unable to understand each other's point of view.

The western system concentrates on specialties and produces technical experts in many diverse fields such as compensation, pensions, design engineering, merchandising, packaging, transportation, capital budgeting, auditing, forecasting, software design, and so on. The list is almost endless. A career path begins with the selection of a function, acquisition of specialized knowledge and expertise in some area within the function, and then, perhaps, some subsequent broadening out into related areas. The lower-middle manager in our system is much like a consultant with specialized knowledge and training. Once again, this system has its advantages and disadvantages. Certainly, job mobility is greatly increased by the possession of a needed specialty. A good pensions manager can probably move from one company to another and be effective in a short period of time, as can any number of other "specialized" managers. Because our organizations are set up around specialties, people can move in and out of jobs with a minimum of fuss, and we are able to hire individuals with proven success records in other firms and put their expertise to work directly in our own company.

Moving from one job to another and one function to another, as we know from our earlier discussions, places tremendous demands on an individual. Despite the common denominators in each specialized area, jobs can differ considerably. They often require a different style of leadership, motivation, communication, and decision-making, and they sometimes require difficult personal adjustments to manage them effectively. Here our strong sense of individualism puts us at a disadvantage, because we have to handle these problems alone. The group-oriented Japanese, on the other hand, are able to cope with a move from one job to a very different one with less difficulty because they have the support of the group to help them make the transition. Also, they are not expected to reach 100 percent productivity right away; the organization provides them with a cushion of experience and expertise within the group and is willing to let them develop into the new job. After all, they're there for life, so time is not a critical factor.

The western cultures value job mobility highly. It is a safety net and it allows us to maintain a sense of independence. The route to high job mobility appears to be through specialization, and we make career choices at an early age. The education system in North America encourages these early choices by streaming curricula. A young person has to choose between *A* and *B,* and once the choice is made it's difficult to backtrack. Once we enter a job and are embarked on a career in a specific function, we become locked in even more tightly. A change in careers that involves moving to another major functional area often means starting at the bottom again. Our view of organizations tends to be vertical rather than horizontal, and this causes problems when it comes to coordinating the activities of different functional groups. One of the great weaknesses in western organizations is their inability to make effective horizontal linkages.

Western businesses could probably overcome the problems of specialization if they wanted to by implementing systems of job rotation early in the careers of managers. We know that job movement is difficult, often traumatic, but it is certainly easier for the young than the old, and if it's to be done, then it should be done early. The problem is the great resistance to such programs from the individuals concerned who feel they aren't gaining any specific expertise and therefore aren't acquiring any increased value in the marketplace. Generalization is perceived as a device that removes mobility and independence, and although it may be accepted in the short term as basic training, the young trainee soon wants to know when he or she is going to be given a "proper" job in which a specialty may be learned.

The problem of generalization for western industries is twofold. First, it goes against the grain of individualism, and secondly it's difficult to cope with in an environment where results are expected very shortly after an individual moves into a job. We don't know if there is a Japanese equivalent to the Peter Principle. Perhaps the support systems provided by the strong group-oriented atmosphere help most people overcome the difficulties of coping with new and different jobs. Maybe the weaker individuals merely pass through them into something they can cope with better. But we know the Peter Principle exists in our organizations, and we see examples of it daily. We know that if you don't make the proper adjustments in style or job and you don't produce results in the relatively short run, you could be looking at the end of the line in your organization. It's an unpleasant situation. We aren't going to change our cultural values overnight: independence and individuality are still going to be prized. But we can help solve the problem of the Peter Principle.

M.ach One can help you look at a new job to see how it should best be managed, and it can help you look at yourself to see what you can and should do differently. We don't have to make futile attempts to copy managerial systems that are rooted in a culture completely different from ours. We can still play our game, only we hope we can play it better.

Equality of Opportunity vs. Hierarchical Stratification

A final basic difference between the cultures of the West and Japan—and the one that best argues against the possibility of transposing Japanese management methods to the West—is the emphasis on equality of opportunity versus Japan's hierarchical stratification. By hierarchical stratification we mean a system in which one's position and role are determined by a number of forces largely outside of one's control, and where mobility within the system, outside the preordained paths, is difficult. In Japan, admission into the right kindergarten at age three or four can determine one's career. A diploma from a prestigious university guarantees a job with a prestigious firm. Being non-Japanese or female means having little or no chance of a managerial career. A young and promising managerial candidate must wait up to ten years before his performance is evaluated and it is decided whether he will advance on the basis of his skill and ability. There is no mechanism to speed up this process. Patience and humility are necessary qualities in a young employee.

We have a much lower tolerance for rigidity of social and organizational structure. It is a fundamental belief in North America that all people are created equal, that all have a chance to become president, that success is largely a result of what you do rather than who you know. Life may not be that way in actuality, but we still like to believe it is, or more importantly, that it should be. Our society holds individual freedom and equality of opportunity as important goals. Despite the initial defeat of the Equal Rights Amendment, women are occupying, and will occupy, more and more places of power and authority in North American business. The majority of college students in the United States are now women; a third of all masters students in business administration are female. We cannot claim to be a totally nondiscriminatory society, but we would like to be. Legislation has ensured that minorities have an equal chance in business and elsewhere. Equality of opportunity is our corollary of the desire for individuality and independence.

Much of the managerial practice in Japan is based on hierarchical structuring in which certain classes of people have specified roles and positions. There is less potential for mobility. The system of lifetime employment, given such fanfare as a cornerstone of the mechanism that begets loyalty and commitment from employees, is made possible largely because women are almost universally considered "temporary" employees and are automatically laid off when business turns down. The role of women in Japanese business is to act as a buffer against economic fluctuation. By the same token, ethnic minorities have little chance of succeeding in Japan. The top jobs are the property of the "hometown boys."

A major force opposing the implementation of a truly Japanese approach to management in our culture is our desire to be rewarded for what we do, not on the basis of who we are, who we know, or what school we went to. We are unwilling to accept strictures on social movement. We believe anybody can become successful if they have the talent and the drive, and we see examples by the thousands around us every day. All we ask is the opportunity to "show our stuff." And once we have, we want to know how we've done, and we want to know right away, not five or ten years later. We don't like to be told to be patient and that all will be well in time. Equality of opportunity is a fundamental right that we are willing to, and will continue to, fight for, and we're unlikely to accept a system that takes that away from us.

CAN WE MANAGE LIKE THE JAPANESE?

William Ouchi, the author of *Theory Z,* contrasts the Japanese and American approaches to management and organization and identifies the salient characteristics of Japanese organizations as:

- Lifetime employment
- Slow evaluation and promotion
- Nonspecialized career paths
- Implicit control mechanisms
- Collective decision-making
- Collective responsibility
- Wholistic concern for people and organizations

He argues that if we are to be more successful, we should try to develop some of these characteristics. His basic argument is that we need more commitment from employees, a less selfish, individualistic approach to work, greater trust, a higher degree of loyalty to the organization and its goals, more openness and cooperation, and less emphasis on status and authority differences. Who can disagree with that? The proposal sounds ideal. The question is, to what degree is it feasible? Is it based on sound assumptions about the nature of people, jobs and organizations *in our culture,* and will it work?

Lifetime Employment

The argument in support of lifetime employment is that employees no longer have to worry about job security, and as a result they have a greater degree of trust in the organization, identify more with its goals and objectives, and are more committed to them. Lifetime employment is a "contract" between the individual and the organization whereby the former promises support and the latter promises good performance.

The system in Japan, however, is based on several practices that are perhaps not commonly known. First a significant percentage of salary is paid in the form of a bonus (35–50 percent is not uncommon), and therefore when productivity and profits are down, the bonus forms a large cushion that can be cut. Wages and salaries are more of a variable cost than they are in the West. Secondly, as mentioned above, women are used as a buffer against downturns, and as "temporary" employees are laid off in poor times.

Our experiences with profit sharing have generally not been good. Workers are reluctant to share in losses. And in organizations where there is virtually a lifetime employment contract—that is, where layoffs and firings are almost unheard of, as in many government bureaucracies and some large utilities—rather than finding a workforce that is highly committed to achievement, we find people who do as little as possible while they milk the system for all it's worth. The test of "guaranteed" employment systems has apparently failed in North America. Given the structure of our economy and the values of the individuals within it, it is simply not practical. Such a system is workable when the economic climate is on the upswing, but we don't have the built-in buffers to sustain it in hard times.

Slow Evaluation and Promotion

The Japanese system of slow evaluation and promotion is based on the idea that it takes time to develop skills and abilities, that loyalty and commitment need to be subjected to a proper period of testing, and that if one has a long time to work before being specifically evaluated, the factors on which you will be evaluated will be the important ones that make real contributions, not just the flashy short-term ideas that look attractive at the moment. The arguments for this type of system are compelling, but it is unlikely that an achievement-oriented individual will be willing to wait for ten years or so before his or her performance is singled out for reward. High achievers want to know how they're doing as quickly as possible. They want to have timely and clear evaluations of performance so that they can make any changes necessary in order to achieve the best results. They are competitive and interested in doing things on their own, taking full responsibility, and savoring the full thrill of victory when they succeed. They're not great team players, but they're willing to take challenges and risks and put their all into a job. After ten years without feedback, none of them would still be in their jobs.

One of the more powerful motivational tools available to western managers is positive reinforcement—that is, noting good performance and rewarding it instantaneously, usually in a nonmonetary fashion. It's a widely used technique, and the results leave no doubt that people like to be recognized and praised for doing a good job. And, in our culture, they like to be praised *as individuals*. We see ourselves more as separate and individual entities than do the Japanese, and we require support that is aimed at that individuality. Rather than slow evaluation and promotion, rapid feedback and reward tied to performance tend to have more positive results for us.

We've already looked at the issue of specialization vs. generalization and seen that in the West we tend to use specialization as a means of upward movement and job mobility. All organizations certainly need managers with a general view of operations, and problems definitely arise from the tunnel vision that is a common characteristic of one who spends his life in one specialized area of the firm. However, a changeover from specialization to generalization needs to be accompanied by a change in the total reward system, and these rewards must be seen to outweigh the potential disadvantages of a loss of "expertise," and therefore market value and job mobility. The concept is certainly not unknown in North America. Exxon moves its managers around through many functions and areas, the rationale being that the company is highly diverse and one needs an overall grasp of its many facets to be able to manage effectively. There's nothing wrong with this sort of policy, but the individuals in the organization need to feel that the moves are beneficial to them as well as to the organization, and they have to feel that the moves represent "advances." We know the trauma that accompanies many job changes—there must be some adequate compensation for it.

From an organizational point of view, it is essential that jobs and individuals be matched carefully when moves are planned. The objective should be to provide an individual with a job that challenges him or her, but not to the point that it makes the individual snap. We can all increase our behavior range and develop new skills, but because the organization also wants to maintain results and avoid costly failures, some analysis of jobs and individuals can provide a substantial payoff. A degree of generality in training and development is good, but it needs to be approached in a sensible and realistic manner. Remember that our culture doesn't provide a strong group structure and orientation to help people over difficult situations, but we can provide help organizationally by making sure that job assignments fit individuals to some degree.

Implicit Control Mechanisms

It's argued that the Japanese don't need the complex and often cumbersome control systems that exist in our organizations to monitor behavior and performance because their organizations have a philosophy that is understood and accepted by all members. Employees don't need specific objectives, or precise sets of performance targets; they know what fits the organization, what will be considered good or poor performance, and what actions are appropriate in any situation. They are guided by their strong identification with the company philosophy. Needless to say, this type of situation has to be supported by a tremendous amount of communication, formal and informal, between all members of the organization. Since the Japanese never operate alone, but are always in interaction with one another, such communication is possible. Managers in Japan are not simply given jobs and left alone to do them, as are managers in North America. All actions and decisions are taken as a result of discussion, and this constant discussion, over time, leads to a clear understanding of the goals and objectives of the firm. Lifetime employment, a decade to prove oneself, and constant job rotation all reinforce this system of communication.

The basis of the implicit control mechanism in Japanese business is the group. Management is a collectivity, and authority, responsibility, and power are all shared. The system works well, as we have said, if you don't have a strong underlying drive for individualism and competition. But we in the West don't have that inbred cultural sense of organizational loyalty, and there are many times when we want to be told what's required and then left alone to get on with it. Because our culture is *not* homogeneous, we operate much more *situationally*. There may be times when we don't have to, or want to, spell out objectives, but there will also be other times when it is critical to do so. It's naive to think that we can make our organizations into large, happy, families in which everyone thinks alike. This idea just doesn't fit our culture.

Collective Decision-Making and Collective Responsibility

Our discussion of decision-making has indicated that at times decisions are best made by an individual, and at other times they are best made by group consensus. We've also made the point that you can overuse consensus methods. Some people just want to get on with their jobs and not be bothered with decisions that can and should be made elsewhere by others. We curse all the meetings that we have to attend, and the time wasted in them. The Japanese make *all* their decisions on a consensus basis, and it works well for them, but we don't have the tolerance for such a lengthy process of decision-making. There's no doubt that when a decision is made by consensus, there's no problem with acceptance and commitment to it. But since we're far more individualistic, and the people in our organizations have far more diverse views on things, the time it would take for us to always make decisions collectively would be immense.

By the same token, collective responsiblity just doesn't strike us as being "strong." We believe that if you're to be a leader, you have to be able to stand on your own two feet and take responsibility for your actions, as is reflected in our admiration and widespread imitation of Harry Truman's line, "the buck stops here." We admire people who take a position. That's not to say we don't believe in discussion and compromise, but we also believe that there are times when you have to stand up and be counted.

Collective decision-making and collective responsibility are *not* suitable patterns for all of western management. We deal with a wide variety of different people and different situations, and we can't rely on consistent patterns of behavior. Management in the West is situational, and strong task-centered behavior is extremely successful at certain times.

*A Wholistic Concept of People
and Organization*

159
M.ach One as a
Blueprint of
Managerial
Achievement

The literature on Japanese management methods presents nothing that is really new. Everything that is put forward as ''Japanese'' was advocated twenty years ago by people like Warren Bennis, Chris Argyris, Richard Beckhard, Ed Schein, and other behavioral scientists who introduced the concepts of what we now call Organizational Development. They talked about integrating the individual and the organization, about participation, collective approaches to decision-making, and equality in the power structure, and these are the very things that are now said to be attractive elements in Japanese organizations. The feeling of oneness with the organization, involvement, cross-functional communication, openness, candor, and continuing change and challenge in jobs without fear of terrible punishment for mistakes are all concepts advocated to western business in the 1950's and 1960's. The Japanese have simply provided an example of how well these things can work. It's old wine in new bottles.

But what the pioneer organizational development theorists failed to recognize was the incredibly important effect of culture on behavior in organizations. The people who work in our organizations are products of our culture and hold the values with which our culture has imbued them. It just so happens that some of these values go strongly against collectivism, group orientation, and the subordination of individualistic competition. Wherever the situation is appropriate, participative, open, shared-management techniques are terrific—just be sure you evaluate the situation correctly. People in western organizations generally don't want to enmesh their lives with their jobs, or swear undying loyalty to the organization. They want to retain a part of themselves for themselves and are often reluctant to be completely open and candid. They want to go head-to-head with someone else and let the best person win. It is extremely important that they preserve their individuality and are able to exercise their own discretion, and they readily accept the consequences of both their mistakes and their victories. Management is a dynamic game—you play the shots according to the lie of the ball and the demands of the hole, and they're always different.

M.ACH ONE AS A BLUEPRINT OF MANAGERIAL ACHIEVEMENT

The M.ach One system is firmly based on the recognition of the cultural influences in the West, that our society is not homogeneous, and that it is susceptible to the winds of change as never before. The organization that hasn't changed over the past five years is in for a rough ride. There have been significant changes in technology, markets, competition, economics, social values, and people. People are becoming more highly educated, and their expectations are altering. The great ''baby boom'' has entered the workforce and organizations are filled with people of roughly similar age, tenure, and experience, so that the opportunity for rapid upward mobility that was made possible in the past by the retirement of older personnel is becoming less widespread. These are times that require thoughtful analysis and a careful situational approach, not mindless pursuit of the latest version of the Holy Grail.

M.ach One is not a philosophy of business; rather, it is a framework within which a philosophy can be implemented. Every successful enterprise needs to have a clear grasp of what its essential business is, what its strengths and weaknesses are, where its major opportunities lie, and where its greatest dangers lurk. It needs to have a good sense of direction, and it needs to communicate that direction to every level. There are many outstanding firms whose foundation on a strong and clear business philosophy has made them successful. And they are as different from one another as chalk and cheese. But they have in common a blend of philosophy and style that fits their particular situation. Although they may look different and often fail to conform to "standard" organizational design and management practice, they do have a design for success, but it's unique to them and not a packaged one that applies universally. They all know that you can't copy what another organization does unless your situation is identical. What's good for GM may not necessarily be what's good for your company. We need to look at the situation, not at a "formula."

THE SITUATION AS THE BASIS FOR MANAGEMENT

Heineken, the Dutch brewing company, maintains about 40 percent of the imported beer market in the United States and 60 percent of its home market in the Netherlands. Its success is based on a philosophy that stresses quality above all. Freddy Heineken takes his beer seriously. "I make the Rolls Royce of beers," he told a *Fortune* reporter, "I consider a bad bottle of beer to be a personal insult to me." The dedication to quality is all-pervasive in Heineken, and the owner's pride in his name and his product is clear to everyone in the organization. The company has a strong and coherent strategy that flows from this emphasis on quality and freshness, and it has far surpassed its competitors. But Heineken's organizational structure is rather unique; it has three managing directors, each of whom has direct responsibility for a geographic area of the world and staff responsibility for certain functions across the board. Freddy Heineken himself is president and Chief Executive Officer, and owns more than 50 percent of the company. His influence is felt everywhere, and his devotion to the company and his conception of quality have an extremely strong effect on the styles of his managers. They have to be, as he phrases it, "disciples"; after that's established, the way management is structured isn't important.

One of the great business success stories in North America is certainly that of Crown Cork and Seal, which has a record of increased earnings each year extending back some twenty-five years. It competes against giants more than three times its size, yet outperforms them consistently. The company, under the guidance of John F. Connelly, has developed a clear, concise, and consistent philosophy of business. That philosophy centers around remaining relatively small and lean, concentrating on the manufacture of certain types of technologically complex packages, avoiding basic research and development, focusing on customer service, setting demanding goals, rewarding good performance, and refusing to tolerate poor performance. In its pursuit of excellence, the company openly states it is willing to tolerate a high level of executive turnover. This is a no-nonsense, high-performance company, doing business in one of the most competitive industries in the world, against firms much larger and richer than it is—and Crown Cork is incredibly successful at it. The style is far from Japanese. Problems are immediate, performance is rated in the short term as well as the long term, everyone has to be on his toes, awake, and running hard to stay ahead of the ever-present competition and to cope with the pressures of customers who are always trying to squeeze margins. Who said lifetime employment and collective responsibility were the only way to go? What about good old American initiative and drive?

What do you think of a company whose philosophy is based on statements like these?

- Competition is the foundation of man's development. It is the spur that makes progress.

- Competition means that there will be losers as well as winners in the game. Competition will mean the disappearance of the lazy and the incompetent, be they workers, industrialists, or distributors.

- There should be an overall bonus based on the contribution each person makes to efficiency. If each person is properly rated and paid, there will not only be a fair reward to each worker, but friendly and exciting competition.

- The incentives that are most potent when properly offered are: money in proportion to production, status as a reward for achievement, publicity of the worker's contributions and skill.

Would you be able to decide whether this was a successful or unsuccessful company, or whether it had high or low employee turnover if you heard employees making remarks like the following?

- I believe in being my own man. I want to use my drive for my own gain.

- The thing I don't like is having to depend on other people on the line.

- You're responsible for your own work, and you even put your stencil on every machine you work on. That way, if it breaks down in the field and they have to take it back, they know who's responsible.

- They don't give anything away. You work for it.

Would you alter your opinion if you knew this company is located in the Midwest, has no air-conditioning in its plant, on occasion makes overtime mandatory, makes arbitrary job reassignments when business is slack, regardless of seniority, and refuses to let any senior executives talk to the press?

This is the Lincoln Electric Company. It has not laid off an employee since 1951. It guarantees a thirty-hour week for all employees with more than two years of seniority. Earnings have increased ten times over the last twenty years. It has a 19 percent return on equity. In most years it pays its workers bonuses that average 100 percent of base pay. And a product that sold for $1,550 more than *sixty-five* years ago now sells for about $1,000. How's *that* for achievement?

On the other hand, how successful do you think a company will be if its philosophy is based on the following five assertions?

- All people are good.
- People, workers, management, and company are all the same thing.
- Every single person in a company must understand the essence of the business.
- Every employee must benefit from the company's success.
- You must create an environment in which all of the above must happen.

Would you find it easier to decide if you knew that there is a company swimming pool and patio, a company jogging trail and exercise facilities, a weekly beer party every Friday at poolside to which every employee is invited, periodic weekend company barbecues for employees working overtime, and a president who states that "Most people need less management than you think"? What if you knew that every employee has to read a book entitled *Understanding Our Philosophy* and attend a two-day course on it, and that the company goes to great lengths to ensure that everyone, management and nonmanagement alike, understands the essence of the company's business and its plans for the next five years? And what if you heard a senior manager saying, "Controls are not a lot of reviews or meetings or reports, but rather the control is understanding the basic concept and philosophy"? Are you getting the feeling that this isn't a western company? Could this be a Japanese one, or at least a Japanese company located in the West?

The company is Tandem Computers Inc., with headquarters in Cupertino, California, or Silicon Valley as it is more widely known. Its sales doubled two years ago, have jumped in the last year from about $200 million to over $300 million, and are expected to reach $1 billion in three years. It earns 12–13 percent on sales and provides about a 10 percent return on investment. As we see once again, our culture allows very different approaches, all of which can be highly successful if they're designed appropriately for the situation.

None of the companies cited have used M.ach One. They have managed, in an organizational sense, to match their styles and strategies to the environments in which they operate. The point that they make is that, unlike the Japanese, our culture is heterogeneous enough to allow a wide variety of approaches to work well. Although this is good to know, it also makes things more difficult. If only one approach has to be followed, life is a great deal easier. Since we are faced with a complex and constantly changing environment, we need a means of analyzing alternatives and deciding on the best approach for the time and place.

163
M.ach One as a
Technique for
Increasing
Organizational
Achievement

M.ACH ONE AS A TECHNIQUE FOR INCREASING ORGANIZATIONAL ACHIEVEMENT

M.ach One is a tool and a technique that allows you and your organization to focus on the critical issue of tailoring your approach to management so that it will be congruent with the situation you face, and so that you will be able to get the most out of your skills and abilities. It doesn't offer the ''seven steps to Nirvana''; it doesn't set down a pat formula; it isn't the best western management system or the best eastern management system, either. It simply provides a framework for managers and organizations to use in examining the tasks ahead of them and the human resources that they have to cope with these tasks. M.ach One is as applicable in Japan as it is in the United States or Europe or the Third World countries—it has no cultural bias. It points the way to higher achievement in any situation by indicating the most appropriate ''style'' of management, style being used in its broadest sense as encompassing the entire range of behaviors a manager uses in doing his or her job.

As we have learned, the two critical issues in management style are appropriateness to the situation and consistency. If your approach fits the requirements of the situation and you are consistent in all that you do to implement it, achievement is purely a matter of energy, thoughtfulness, and drive. We know, of course, that all managers aren't created equal; some are brighter than others, or are more skilled than others in certain areas. But where managers differ most is in the way they apply these attributes to their work. You can be highly intelligent, extremely hard-working, energetic, and active, and still fritter away your time doing the wrong things or doing them in an inappropriate and incorrect fashion. M.ach One is designed to help you identify the basic demands and dimensions of your job, take stock of your abilities and shortcomings, and make the best match you can. It's a tried and tested approach that can increase your achievement level dramatically—and, when extended to the people around you, can improve the achievement level of your work group, department, division, and company.

We wish you good luck!

Appendix 1

Managerial Style
Descriptions

The objective of this Appendix is to provide an easily accessible summary of the nine managerial styles for the reader who is interested in applying the M.ach One system to his or her job and organization. The appendix includes:

- The capsule style descriptions from Chapter 3.
- Data on how each of the nine types of managers approach the issues of *creativity, control, conflict,* and *commitment* in their jobs.
- A summary of the behavioral cues for each of the nine managerial styles.

THE TASK-CENTERED STYLES

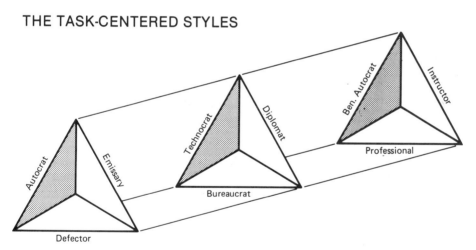

Figure A-1. The Task-Centered Styles

The Benevolent Autocrat (TC +)

The Benevolent Autocrat is task centered and is a high achiever. His prime concern is the completion of any job under his direction. Subordinates sometimes see the Benevolent Autocrat as having a concern for people, but this concern usually takes the form of paternalism, and he exhibits little real openness to the ideas of others. He is firm with people, but is able to engender loyalty and commitment. Subordinates tend to follow his lead with little question. He is completely confident in his ability to get the job done, but less confident in the people around him. As a result, he structures

167

work and attempts to decrease interpersonal relationships. He is concerned with status symbols and other formalized procedures that determine interaction patterns. He tends to "sell" his ideas. He is motivated by the desire to complete his job successfully, no matter what, and if he has to push people out of the way to do so, he will.

CREATIVITY. The Benevolent Autocrat is not overly concerned with creativity. He will not, however, dissuade individuals from attempts at creativity unless these involve a decrease in individual output, even in the short term. The Benevolent Autocrat is principally concerned with the accomplishment of immediate goals. If a new method will achieve the same end, fine, but if results will only be seen somewhere in the more distant future, he is not interested. While he has little concern for creativity, he doesn't allow his subordinates to feel this lack of interest. He will humour them as long as they get the job done, on time and on target.

CONTROL. Control is central to the BA style. The ability to control and direct without creating open hostility on the part of subordinates is a major prerequisite of task-centered high achievement. The Benevolent Autocrat exerts control through information. He makes sure he has access to all important information concerning the work of his unit, and he spends a great deal of his time gathering and evaluating that information. The BA is able to exert pressure *only when necessary* simply because he knows exactly what's going on at all times. Subordinates know that he will not push them if he is sure they're producing the results expected of them, and they also know that if they fall behind in their work they can expect to hear about it. It's this sense of a combination of fairness and discipline that gets subordinates to work hard for a BA boss.

CONFLICT. There is little open conflict in a work unit headed by a Benevolent Autocrat, since subordinates are unsure as to whether they fear him or respect him. But they are sure that it is dangerous to cross him. The BA tries never to allow conflict to develop because it would weaken his position and possibly result in a lessening of control. Because he always tries to maintain control, he feels that disagreement should be dealt with early, and he attempts to tell how, when, and where to do a job, but not necessarily why. Conflict based on the "why" of a job is usually brushed aside on the basis that it is part of an overall design of which the individual subordinate is not fully aware. This hearkens back to his habit of controlling information and only allowing subordinates to know as much as he wants them to know.

COMMITMENT. The Benevolent Autocrat is committed first and foremost to the task at hand. He is also committed to those subordinates who follow his directives and who get the results he requires. Those who wish to take a more independent route find him very hard to work for, and usually end up being moved somehow. His methods are smooth and effective, and he tends to develop a very high commitment to organizational objectives among his subordinates. He sets an example by his own dedication and hard work, and expects others to emulate it. If they do, they can expect his full and unconditional support; if they don't they can expect to be subjected to a great deal of pressure.

The Technocrat (TC 0)

The Technocrat is task-centered, but is a moderate rather than a high achiever. He is, however, more effective than the Autocrat in that he is more subtle in introducing his one-sided philosophy. He often hides behind various statistical and technological data, convincing people that his arguments have merit. He is usually cool, calm, and collected. Normally ultra-prepared, he is a hard person to argue against. Subordinates or co-workers often rationalize any hostility they feel toward his actions as being a fault of the technology in general, rather than him personally. The Technocrat might be more effective if he did not make people feel so replaceable. Sometimes he creates fear in others when he pushes for new methods and ideas they don't fully understand.

The Technocrat's motivation is variable—sometimes he is motivated to help the organization, while at other times he is motivated to satisfy his own whims. He prefers to interact with technology rather than people. He is often happiest when left alone with machines and data.

The prevalence of this management style is growing, due to rapid advances in technology. The result, in many cases, is a fragile equilibrium of opposing forces between the status quo (the so-called organizational establishment) and the young, technically trained graduates who are armed with new concepts and techniques that may be threatening to those unfamiliar with them.

CREATIVITY. While he supports creative ideas and is often the first person to adopt new techniques, technology, and systems, the Technocrat is not usually the individual who has developed these innovative advances. This lack of personal creativity may come about because he enjoys the application of new techniques so much that he doesn't have time to actually invent or develop anything himself. His essential task-centeredness keeps him focused on getting results by using the available technology, but because he is not highly organizationally oriented, he is not concerned about making significant improvements that might increase output or achievement.

CONTROL. The Technocrat exerts control by making his systems and technology complex and slightly mystical. He guards the "secrets" of such things as computer technology and surrounds them with technical jargon, making it very difficult for outsiders to penetrate his screen. He then uses others' ignorance of the workings of his systems to control them. His achievement level is neutral because people are aware of his game and sometimes react negatively to it.

CONFLICT. The Technocrat attempts to avoid conflict because he feels incapable of handling people who are emotional and upset. He focuses on "the facts and nothing but the facts" and assures himself that a purely logical approach will ultimately lead to reconciliation. His own emotional reaction in a conflict situation is one of exasperation at the inability of others to see the logic and rationality of his arguments.

COMMITMENT.   The Technocrat is committed to the mechanics of his job. His task-centeredness is channelled towards getting things designed and run properly, almost regardless of whether that is good or bad for the organization. Sometimes his systems and techniques are highly appropriate to organizational needs, in which case his achievement is positive, but at other times they are overly elaborate or simply do not meet these needs, and his contributions serve to decrease overall results.

The Autocrat (TC —)

The Autocrat is task-centered, but a low achiever. He has a single purpose—to get the job done at any cost. It should be noted that his task-centeredness is focused on what *he* wants to have done, rather than what the organization wants to have done, and his behavior is more a manifestation of his personality than a response to the needs of the situation. People are of interest to him only insofar as they can further his goals. This single-mindedness and insensitivity to others is ineffective in the long term because people will only work for him when the pressure is great enough, and will tend to slack off when he is not pressuring them. The net result is not conducive to organizational achievement.

The Autocrat is a bully. Unlike the Benevolent Autocrat who is able to command loyalty and commitment from subordinates, the Autocrat simply engenders fear and dislike. He is highly self-oriented. His behavior focuses on achieving his own goals over those of the organization.

In the Autocrat's view, people dislike work and must be pressured or punished in order to perform. Any decrease in expected results calls for an increase in threats and demands. "Shape up or ship out" is his motto. He does not believe that a subordinate can be motivated to work by himself without close direction.

CREATIVITY.   The Autocrat has no interest in creativity. Creativity means that something is not being done his way. As far as he is concerned, subordinates should take orders and carry them out without question and without deviation.

CONTROL.   Control is absolutely essential to the Autocrat. It is his obsession, and he demands absolute authority over others. He always supervises very closely and believes that most organizational ills can be attributed to a loose rein on personnel.

CONFLICT.   Conflict is seen by the Autocrat as a sign of weakness. If orders are specific and clear, and subordinates are watched closely, conflict should not arise. If it should rear its ugly head, the Autocrat is quick to stamp it out with vigor. Conflict is insubordination and must be dealt with swiftly and severely.

COMMITMENT. The Autocrat shows little commitment to the organization. His commitment is to getting his own way and exercising his own personal power. He has his own views as to how things should be done and he expends all his effort making sure that others conform.

THE SITUATION-CENTERED STYLES

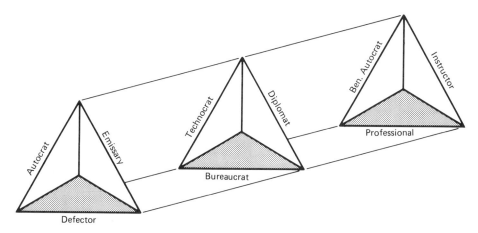

Figure A-2. The Situation-Centered Styles

The Professional (SC +)

The Professional is a high achiever who views his job as "getting things done through people". His situation-centeredness is manifested by a great deal of effort toward integration, coordination, and synthesis of the efforts of others. He is highly concerned about people *and* about getting the job done well, and he becomes deeply involved in his efforts to ensure that both these aspects of work are handled properly. He is a good delegator, listener, and team player, yet will make decisions himself when required.

The Professional is more interested in establishing strategy and achieving group results than demonstrating individual brilliance. He sets high standards and demands a great deal from himself and those who work with him. He recognizes that a manager must be sensitive to the demands of the job at all times. He sees his function, to a large degree, as the blending of people, skills, and technology to achieve organizational goals. He believes that people can enjoy work and that they find high levels of achievement rewarding. Although he is essentially team oriented, the Professional is careful to treat people as individuals with unique skills and abilities. However, he attempts to structure activities so that achievement is a product of a team effort from which all members can derive satisfaction. He uses knowledge rather than tenure or rank as the criterion for determining who should do what, and has little concern for status. He is not afraid to take a firm stance and to assume a more directive leadership style when necessary.

CREATIVITY. The Professional believes that creativity is the life blood of any successful organization. He encourages it within the groups he manages, channeling the ideas and suggestions of team members toward the solution of organizational problems. The Professional attempts to listen to all ideas presented to him, and to implement those that appear to have merit. When suggestions are not accepted, he makes a point of explaining why to those involved.

CONTROL. The Professional is concerned with control both in terms of task and people. He needs to know the direction that work under his authority is taking, and how the individuals and groups doing it are coping. His concern is to make sure that the right resources are allocated to the right tasks, and that people and jobs complement one another. Control is used as a means of keeping in touch with progress toward objectives, but not as a device for wielding power. The Professional sees control as helpful to all concerned.

CONFLICT. Conflict is accepted as being a natural result of a group of people endeavoring to maximize output. Where both teamwork and individual creativity are expected, differences of opinion are bound to result. The Professional sees it as his job to manage such conflict, making sure that it remains at the level of the job and not of personality, and attempting to channel it towards the creative solution of organizational problems.

COMMITMENT. The Professional is highly committed to his job, his people, and his organization. He strives to create an environment where this feeling of commitment spreads to others. His success is related to his ability to be equally loyal to both his people and his organization. His expectation of high performance from everyone, including himself, is challenging rather than threatening to subordinates and colleagues.

The Bureaucrat (SC 0)

The Bureaucrat is placed at a neutral level of achievement within the M.ach One system because, although he can often get things done, he does not inject the spark of commitment, creativity, and desire that the Professional does. His situation-centeredness is focused on a clear knowledge of rules and procedures and how and when to apply them. He always plays by the rules and is highly concerned about maintaining proper procedure. In fact he is "ruled" by the rules. The Bureaucrat is intrinsically concerned neither with task achievement nor with personal relationships unless they fall within the prescribed bounds of his job. He is more concerned with doing things right than doing the right things.

Although the Bureaucrat's style does not engender high growth, innovation, and dazzling results, it is a stable, anchoring force that provides the organization with a solid foundation. The Bureaucrat does what has to be done, and does it the "proper" way. He is dogged, steadfast, and reliable (although some may say he is stubborn, obstinate, and obstructive).

His organizing ability often helps others to be highly effective. Without people like him to maintain systems, few organizations would be able to function.

CREATIVITY.   There is little place for creativity within the Bureaucrat's scheme of things. You either do things the prescribed (and therefore proper) way, or not at all. He is relatively inflexible in his application of rules and procedures. If there is a way to do something within the existing framework, that's acceptable, but he will not countenance violations of customary procedure.

CONTROL.   Control is imposed by the system and not by the Bureaucrat himself. He sees himself as a loyal servant to the organization and obeys its rules and regulations. He expects others to do the same. Forms, formats, deadlines and other control devices are seen as part of organizational life and the Bureaucrat's efforts to see that they are conformed to should not be construed as personal; it's simply a matter of getting the job done.

CONFLICT.   In the Bureaucrat's view, if the system is good, conflict should not arise. When it does, the Bureaucrat turns to the procedures manual for a judgment and, failing to find anything there, is content to give the explanation that "We've always done it that way." Conflict does not reach a personal level. It is simply a matter of "the book."

COMMITMENT.   The Bureaucrat is deeply committed to the organization. He sees it as his duty to make sure that things run as they are suposed to run, and he can be dogged in his perseverance. He is married to the organization and to its rules—for richer or for poorer, in sickness and in health, till death do them part.

The Defector (SC −)

The Defector, although physically present, is mentally absent. He is a situation-centered nonachiever. The situation-centeredness is concerned with the Defector's *own* situation, not the organization's, but his skill at sensing what is going on around him and manipulating it to his own ends should not be underestimated. His is a situation-centered style because the Defector has to be highly aware of all elements of the organization in order to continue to get away with doing nothing. The negative aspect of his style centers on his attitude of not giving a damn for the organization. He is there to remain warm in the winter, cool in the summer, and to get what he can without having to give anything in return.

Defectors are far more common in large organizations than small ones, probably because there is less available cover to hide behind in the latter. The Defector needs to be able to give the impression of being concerned and working hard when in fact he is doing just the opposite. He is least damaging when he is content to do nothing, and most damaging when he takes out his frustrations and resentment by blocking and sabotaging the various plans and actions of others. The Defector is introspective, and usually sees himself as having been cheated by the organization, and even by life in general. Frequently he is correct. Most Defectors have suffered some major setback in their organizational careers that they feel unable to overcome. Although this may have soured them on life within their organizations, they are often active on the outside in clubs, charities, church, or various hobbies. Defectors are made, not born, and sometimes they can be changed back into high achievers.

CREATIVITY.   The Defector's creativity is channeled into inventing ways of avoiding work, or of sabotaging the system. It is not directed in a positive way either to increasing his own or his work group's level of achievement. Sometimes the Defector uses a burst of creativity to hinder the actions of others and, depending on how well people understand him, he may be able to get away with it.

CONTROL.   The Defector exercises little or no control over subordinates because he has minimal interest in organizational objectives. He allows people to "do their own thing" as long as it doesn't entail him having to do anything. He is often the object of attempts at stringent control and has an abhorrence of it.

CONFLICT.   The Defector is rarely, if ever, caught up in conflict within the organization. He attempts to sidestep all issues of importance and can rarely be pinned down as being solely responsible for any actions. He is skilled at passing the buck, making others share responsibility, and generally making himself blend into the background of a major issue. Even when cornered, he will try not to take a position, and his stance toward conflict is always avoidance.

COMMITMENT.   The Defector is committed to personal survival. He is in the organization, and he plans to stay there until retirement, doing as little as possible. Because he believes that at best the organization doesn't care about him, and at worst is out to get him, he has no sense of loyalty or commitment to it.

THE RELATIONSHIP-CENTERED STYLES

The Instructor (RC +)

The Instructor is a relationship-centered high achiever. His outlook is a long-term one: he trains people for future positions. He turns people with high technical skills into managers. His main interest is the development of others and, through this, the growth of the organization. His approach may be difficult to detect and so his ability sometimes goes unrewarded, but the success of his "pupils" is his recompense. Elements of this style should be found in every manager, but many fear for their own organizational lives and would prefer to be indispensable. Thus, they refuse to train people to take over their function. This is a rather frustrating circumstance for subordinates, who must jump over such a person, or move laterally, to succeed.

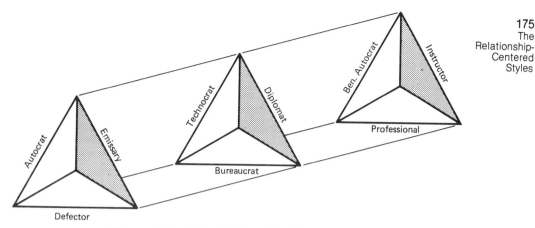

Figure A-3.   The Relationship-Centered Styles

With the training and learning thrust of many modern organizations, the style of the Instructor will become more highly valued. Although formal training programs and "tours of duty" for developmental purposes are being introduced into organizations, a subordinate still gets his best opportunity to learn from a superior who is willing to delegate and to nurture him in new undertakings.

CREATIVITY.   The Instructor fosters a high degree of creativity. He is able to create conditions which provide subordinates with a desire to try new approaches which will increase achievement. He often stretches the organization's formal structure and procedures to allow subordinates more freedom to produce new ideas. He is open to unique and novel thoughts and is willing to tolerate a large number of impractical suggestions on the basis that eventually the process of idea generation will produce something of tangible worth.

CONTROL.   The Instructor does not like control in the formal sense. He believes that managers should exercise self-control and do not need to be monitored closely from above. He feels that an effective manager should have confidence in people, often before their behavior indicates that it is deserved.

CONFLICT.   The Instructor doesn't often find himself in conflict situations. He is too flexible, tolerant and understanding to be forced into a fight. People enjoy learning from him, and when there are differences of opinion, they surface early and are usually settled through discussion and exploration of each point of view. The Instructor attempts to solve disagreements by empathy and logic and does not allow issues to escalate.

COMMITMENT.   The Instructor's commitment is first and foremost to his people. The end result is that his subordinates are well trained and confident in their jobs. His ability shows up in the large numbers of people who have worked under him reaching higher positions in the organization.

The Diplomat (RC 0)

The Diplomat sits on the fence between being a high achiever and a low achiever. He is sometimes one and sometimes the other. Basically relationship-centered, his dealings are with and about people. The difference between the Diplomat and the Instructor is that the Diplomat "uses" people rather than developing them. He is concerned more with self or organization than with the individual. He can be a high achiever as long as people don't catch on to his game, but once they sense they have been used, they react negatively and achievement falls.

His tightrope existence often turns the Diplomat into a compromiser who settles for less than the best solution in order to keep the greatest number of people happy. He is highly political, and very sensitive to the games people play, largely because he tends to be a consummate games-player himself. He is socially fluid, and believes that who you know is more important than what you know. The Diplomat needs to keep moving in order to remain effective, because eventually people recognize him for what he is and react negatively. He can cause very high levels of frustration by his refusal to be tied down to a strong and clear position. A common trait is that he is reluctant to make up his mind on issues, and is influenced by the last person to see him. This can be very upsetting if you happen to have been second to last.

CREATIVITY. The Diplomat sees himself as being highly creative. This creativity is channeled into devising clever moves and strategies in his dealings with people. However, he tends to be more concerned with the short- than the long-term in most of his work relationships, and therefore tends to be inconsistent and somewhat unreliable. He is interested in new ideas, and listens to subordinates' suggestions, but, unlike the Instructor, his concern tends to be more for how these ideas can be used to aid him personally rather than being of help to the individual or organization.

CONTROL. The Diplomat attempts to exert control over others through a complex series of deals, bargains and agreements. He is a political animal, quick to shake the right hand, gregarious, and active. He feels that he has a charismatic aura, and he can become over-awed by his own importance and power. This type of over-confidence can lead to his demise.

CONFLICT. The Diplomat attempts to keep the peace at all times by acting as mediator and compromiser in conflict situations. Sometimes he does so by initiating a series of complex private arrangements with the various parties, creating a somewhat fragile equilibrium. His weakness is that he is willing to accept poor decisions in order to keep the largest number of people happy. His attempts at solving conflict can therefore be either helpful or ultimately harmful, hence his position of neutrality on the achievement scale.

COMMITMENT. The Diplomat's commitment is to a blend of organizational and self-interest. He is happy to solve organizational conflicts and to play the political game in order to increase overall achievement, but there is a very heavy personal agenda at work as well, in that he likes to be at the center of things and a focus of some power and attention.

The Emissary (RC –)

The Emissary is a nonachiever. He is relationship-centered, but only in terms of his own needs. He deludes himself and others into thinking he is concerned about the organization, but his main goal is to be liked by everyone. He sees his role, therefore, as being the purveyor of good news. He thinks it is his duty to keep morale high. The organization should be a pleasant place to be, not necessarily to do work in. If there is a choice to be made between productivity and popularity, he will opt for the latter. His apparent motto is "People are everything," but what he really means is that his personal popularity is everything. The irony is that the Emissary sees himself as being effective, while others may initially see him as being effective, but change their opinions when they realize that the work never gets done.

Like the other negative styles, the Emissary is dominated by his own needs. His personality is one that craves stroking. He has to be liked by everyone; everything else pales by comparison with this need. Unfortunately, he is unable to understand this and sometimes becomes a pitiable figure, making jokes and acting the hail-fellow-well-met character when it is most inappropriate. He is likeable outside the job, but high achievers find him terribly annoying at work.

CREATIVITY. The Emissary is a creative type of "fun and games" leader. He tries to develop an environment where cheer and goodwill prevail. Creativity is limited to keeping people happy, however, and rarely translates into achievement in the job.

CONTROL. The Emissary tries not to indulge in any form of managerial control—that might cause people not to like him. He lacks self-control and is unable to develop priorities and make hard decisions.

CONFLICT. The Emissary cannot abide conflict and will do anything to avoid it. His self-appointed "ministry" is to spread happiness and joy and he uses a philosophy of turning the other cheek as an excuse for not confronting counterproductive behavior. He claims to have an abiding faith in people to do the right thing and sees conflict and argument as somehow challenging the integrity of individuals.

COMMITMENT. The Emissary's stated commitment is to "humanity," but it is in fact to his popularity. He is often willing to sell out the organization's objectives in order to be liked. He won't hand down tough or unpopular directives, and when forced to will make a point of saying that they originated elsewhere.

Key Behavioral Cues for the Nine M.ach One Managerial Styles

THE TASK-CENTERED STYLES

Benevolent Autocrat (TC +)

Dominant	Results-Focus
Firm	Convincing
Initiator	Resolute
Challenge-Oriented	Compelling
	Determined

Technocrat (TC 0)

Logical	Rational
Prepared	Knowledgeable
Technical-Focus	Unemotional
Single-Minded	Orderly

Autocrat (TC −)

Censuring	Dictatorial
Demanding	Pressuring
Hard	Insensitive
Taskmaster	Uses
Bully	Ultimatums

THE SITUATION-CENTERED STYLES

Professional (SC +)

Integrates	Team Player
Fair	Assured
Situation-Sensitive	Strategy-Focus
Coordinates	High Standards

Bureaucrat (SC 0)

Loyal	Careful
Conservative	Impersonal
System-Bound	Fastidious
Detail-Emphasis	Consistent
Routine-Focus	

Defector (SC −)

Uninterested	Unmotivated
Bitter	Devious
Uncooperative	Disillusioned
Irresponsible	Uncommitted

THE RELATIONSHIP-CENTERED STYLES

Instructor (RC +)

Understanding	Educates
Encouraging	Candid
Trains	Listens
Nurtures	Trusting
Open	Coaches
Guides	

Diplomat (RC 0)

Active	Compromiser
Agreeable	Manipulator
Mediator	Sociable
Polished	Political
Joiner	Visible

Emissary (RC −)

Amusing	Irresponsible
Chummy	Weak
Cloying	Optimistic
Indecisive	Harmony-Oriented
Brotherly	

Appendix 2

Managing Style
Location Test (MSLT)

Following is the full-length version of the Managing Style Location Test for those readers who want more detailed feedback on their managerial styles. To receive a computer printout of your scores and an interpretation of your style, complete and detach *all 7 pages* of the test, enclose check or money order for $5 payable to Reston Publishing Company, and mail to the following address:

Rick Roskin
Reston Publishing Company
11480 Sunset Hills Road
Reston, VA 22090

MANAGING STYLE LOCATION TEST (MSLT)

This test is designed as a self-perception instrument and tests how you as a manager perceive your own behavior. It does *not* test how others perceive your behavior. As this test is for your own information and benefit, it should be answered as accurately as possible. Try to recall what you actually think and do in relation to your present job.

Note: *The following is strictly confidential and will be used for research purposes only. Fill out only what you wish.*

Personal Data *(Please print)*

Name _____ Age _____ Sex _____

Employed by _____

Industry Type _____ Your Position _____

How many people do you manage? _____

How long have you been in your present position? _____

Your formal education _____

What formal management training have you had? _____

_____

Address to which results are to be mailed _____

_____

_____

Phone (   ) _____

Thank you.

Instructions

Each of the next four pages contain nine statements. They are arranged in the following format:

		A	B	C	D	E	F	G	H	No. of circled numbers	
1.	I enjoy work	(1) 2	1 (3)	1 4	1 5	1 6	1 7	1 8	1 9	9	
2.	I help subordinates	2 3	2 4	2 5	2 6	2 7	2 8	2 9		8	
3.	I follow rules carefully	3 4	3 5	3 6	3 7	3 8	3 9			7	

Begin by reading statement 1. Compare it to statement 2. In Column A across from number 1 statement is a box containing a 1 and a 2. Circle either 1 or 2 depending upon which is the most accurate description of yourself. In the example above the reader felt that statement 1 described him more closely than 2. Now move across to the next box under Column B. Here you are to compare statement 1 to statement 3. (e.g. the reader felt that 3 was a more accurate description of himself than 1.) Continue to move across making the appropriate comparisons and circling the number that indicates your answer. When you have compared statement 1 to 9 in H Column, move DOWN to statement 2 row and proceed as before (see arrows). **Disregard the "No. of circled numbers" column which will be used after you have completed the test.** You must make a choice in each instance although neither choice may be your preferred answer.

NOTE: It is helpful to place your thumb beside the statement row upon which you are working.

		A	B	C	D	E	F	G	H	No. of circled numbers (Page 1)
1.	I sometimes find it necessary to watch subordinates closely.	1 2	1 3	1 4	1 5	1 6	1 7	1 8	1 9	9
2.	I normally let subordinates resolve their own problems.	2 3	2 4	2 5	2 6	2 7	2 8	2 9		8
3.	I make the maintenance of morale a major part of my job.	3 4	3 5	3 6	3 7	3 8	3 9			7
4.	I use the latest technology to solve company problems.	4 5	4 6	4 7	4 8	4 9				6
5.	I usually follow organizational procedures.	5 6	5 7	5 8	5 9					5
6.	People think I am interested in their personal problems.	6 7	6 8	6 9						4
7.	I see to it that subordinates are working to their capacity.	7 8	7 9							3
8.	I work with subordinates to determine standards of performance.	8 9								2
9.	I enjoy "coaching" subordinates.									1
										36 TOTAL

NOTE: There should only be one circled number per box.

		A	B	C	D	E	F	G	H	No. of circled numbers (Page 2)
1.	I help subordinates with their work.	1 2	1 3	1 4	1 5	1 6	1 7	1 8	1 9	9
2.	I emphasize the "quality" of work turned out.	2 3	2 4	2 5	2 6	2 7	2 8	2 9		8
3.	I push for production as hard as I can and try not to antagonize people.	3 4	3 5	3 6	3 7	3 8	3 9			7
4.	It's wise to join popular movements in the organization.	4 5	4 6	4 7	4 8	4 9				6
5.	I like to attack a problem like I did in the past.	5 6	5 7	5 8	5 9					5
6.	I do not allow emotions to distort logical problem-solving.	6 7	6 8	6 9						4
7.	I make the personal lives of my subordinates part of my interest.	7 8	7 9							3
8.	I have noted that much information crossing my path is of little relevance.	8 9								2
9.	I have observed that many people basically dislike work.									1
										36
										TOTAL

NOTE: There should only be one circled number per box.

		A	B	C	D	E	F	G	H		No. of circled numbers (Page 3)
1.	It seems that many people prefer not to assume increasing responsibility.	1 2	1 3	1 4	1 5	1 6	1 7	1 8	1 9		9
2.	I am sometimes treated like a machine.	2 3	2 4	2 5	2 6	2 7	2 8	2 9			8
3.	I discourage arguments within my group.	3 4	3 5	3 6	3 7	3 8	3 9				7
4.	Where organizational objectives conflict, I try to appease all sides.	4 5	4 6	4 7	4 8	4 9					6
5.	I follow the routine as outlined.	5 6	5 7	5 8	5 9						5
6.	I am sensitive to the kinds of authority possessed by others.	6 7	6 8	6 9							4
7.	I stress being ahead of competing groups.	7 8	7 9								3
8.	I allow others to share in decision-making.	8 9									2
9.	I make the training of my subordinates a significant part of my duties.										1
											36
											TOTAL

NOTE: There should only be one circled number per box.

186
Managing Style
Location Test
(MSLT)

		A	B	C	D	E	F	G	H	No. of circled numbers (Page 4)	
1.	I give guidance to my subordinates.	1 2	1 3	1 4	1 5	1 6	1 7	1 8	1 9	9	
2.	I set very high standards for myself and others.	2 3	2 4	2 5	2 6	2 7	2 8	2 9		8	
3.	I try to convince subordinates as to how a task should be done and who should do it.	3 4	3 5	3 6	3 7	3 8	3 9			7	
4.	I emphasize my own group's success where organizational objectives conflict.	4 5	4 6	4 7	4 8	4 9				6	
5.	I follow organizational lines and approaches.	5 6	5 7	5 8	5 9					5	
6.	I sometimes put more faith in machines than people.	6 7	6 8	6 9						4	
7.	I smooth over conflict whenever it arises.	7 8	7 9							3	
8.	I am sometimes indifferent to organizational policy.	8 9								2	
9.	I emphasize the "quantity" of work turned out.									1	
										36	
										TOTAL	

NOTE: There should only be one circled number per box.

Name: _____

Address: _____

ANALYSIS

After completing the test do the following:

1. On the right hand side of the statement pages are boxes numbered 1 to 9, titled "No. of circled numbers column".

2. Count the number of circled numbers for each number from 1 to 9 on each page and place the figure in the associated "No. of circled numbers box". For example, if the number of circled 1's on the WHOLE PAGE is 6, then 6 should be placed in box 1 at the bottom of the "No. of circled numbers" column. Next count the number of 2's. Continue until you have determined the number of circled numbers for each number from 1 to 9.

3. Add the figures in the column titled "No. of circled numbers". The sum should be 36. If it is not, check your addition. **If the number still does not equal 36, check your circled numbers for errors.**

4. Now transfer the results from the "No. of circled numbers" columns for each of pages 1 to 4 to the RESULTS TABLE below.

RESULTS TABLE

INPUT				
NO.	PAGE 1	PAGE 2	PAGE 3	PAGE 4
9				
8				
7				
6				
5				
4				
3				
2				
1				

Bibliography

Readers who are interested in pursuing further some of the topics discussed in this book, or who may wish to know the antecedents of the thinking behind M.ach One, will find the following list of publications a useful starting point. This is certainly far from a complete list of the works upon which we have drawn in the development of M.ach One, and we apologize in advance to those whose writings and teachings we have not included here. Like any book in the field of management, ours can claim to be about 20% original and 80% based on earlier work.

Bass, B. M. *Stogdill's Handbook of Leadership*. New York: The Free Press, 1981.

Blake, R. R., & Mouton, J. S. *The Managerial Grid*. Houston: Gulf, 1964.

Drucker, P. F. *Managing for Results*. New York: Harper & Row, 1964.

Fiedler, F. E. *A Theory of Leadership Effectiveness*. New York: McGraw-Hill, 1967.

Fleishman, E. A., Harris, E. F., & Burtt, E. H. *Leadership and Supervision in Industry*. Ohio: Bureau of Business Research, Ohio State University, Monograph No. 33, 1955.

Fleishman, E. A., & Hunt, J. G. *Current Developments in the Study of Leadership*. Illinois: Carbondale Southern Illinois University Press, 1973.

Hall, J. "What makes a manager good, bad, or average," *Psychology Today,* August 1976, 52-55.

Hersey, P., & Blanchard, H. *Management of Organizational Behavior*. Englewood Cliffs, N.J.: Prentice-Hall, 1969.

House, R. J. "A path goal theory of leader effectiveness," *Administrative Science Quarterly*, 1971, 16(3), 321:338.

Kepner, C. H., & Tregoe, B. B. *The Rational Manager*, New York: McGraw-Hill, 1965.

Maier, N. R. F. *Problem Solving Discussions and Conferences: Leadership Methods and Skills*. New York: McGraw-Hill, 1963.

Maier, N. R. F. *Problem Solving and Creativity in Individuals and Groups*. Belmont, California: Brooks-Cole, 1970.

Margerison, C. J. *Managerial Problem Solving*. London: McGraw-Hill, 1974.

Maslow, A. H. *Motivation and Personality*. New York: Harper & Row, 1954.

Herzberg, F., Mausner, B., & Snaylerman, B. *The Motivation to Work*. New York: Wiley, 1959.

Korda, M. *Power: How to Get It, How to Use It*. New York: Random House, 1975.

Mackenzie, R. A. *The Time Trap*. New York: McGraw-Hill, 1972.

McClelland, D. C. *The Achieving Society*. Princeton, N.J.: Van Nostrand, 1961.

McGregor, D. *The Human Side of Enterprise*. New York: McGraw-Hill, 1960.

Odiorne, G. S. *Management by Objectives: A System of Managerial Leadership*. Englewood Cliffs, N.J.: Prentice-Hall, 1965.

Ouchi, W. G. *Theory Z*. Reading, Mass.: Addison-Wesley, 1981.

Pascale, R. T., & Athos, A. G. *The Art of Japanese Management*. New York: Simon & Schuster, 1981.

Reddin, W. J. *Managerial Effectiveness*. New York: McGraw-Hill, 1970.

Reddin, W. J. *Effective Management by Objectives*. New York: McGraw-Hill, 1971.

Sloan, A. P. *My Years with General Motors*. Garden City, N.J.: Doubleday, 1963.

Terkel, S. *Working*. New York: Random House, 1974.

Peter, L. J., & Hull, R. *The Peter Principle*. New York: William Morrow, 1969.

Vroom, V. H. & Yetton, P. W. *Leadership and Decision-Making*. Pittsburgh, Pa.: University of Pittsburgh Press, 1973.

Yoshino, M. Y. *Japan's Managerial System*. Boston: M.I.T. Press, 1968.

Index